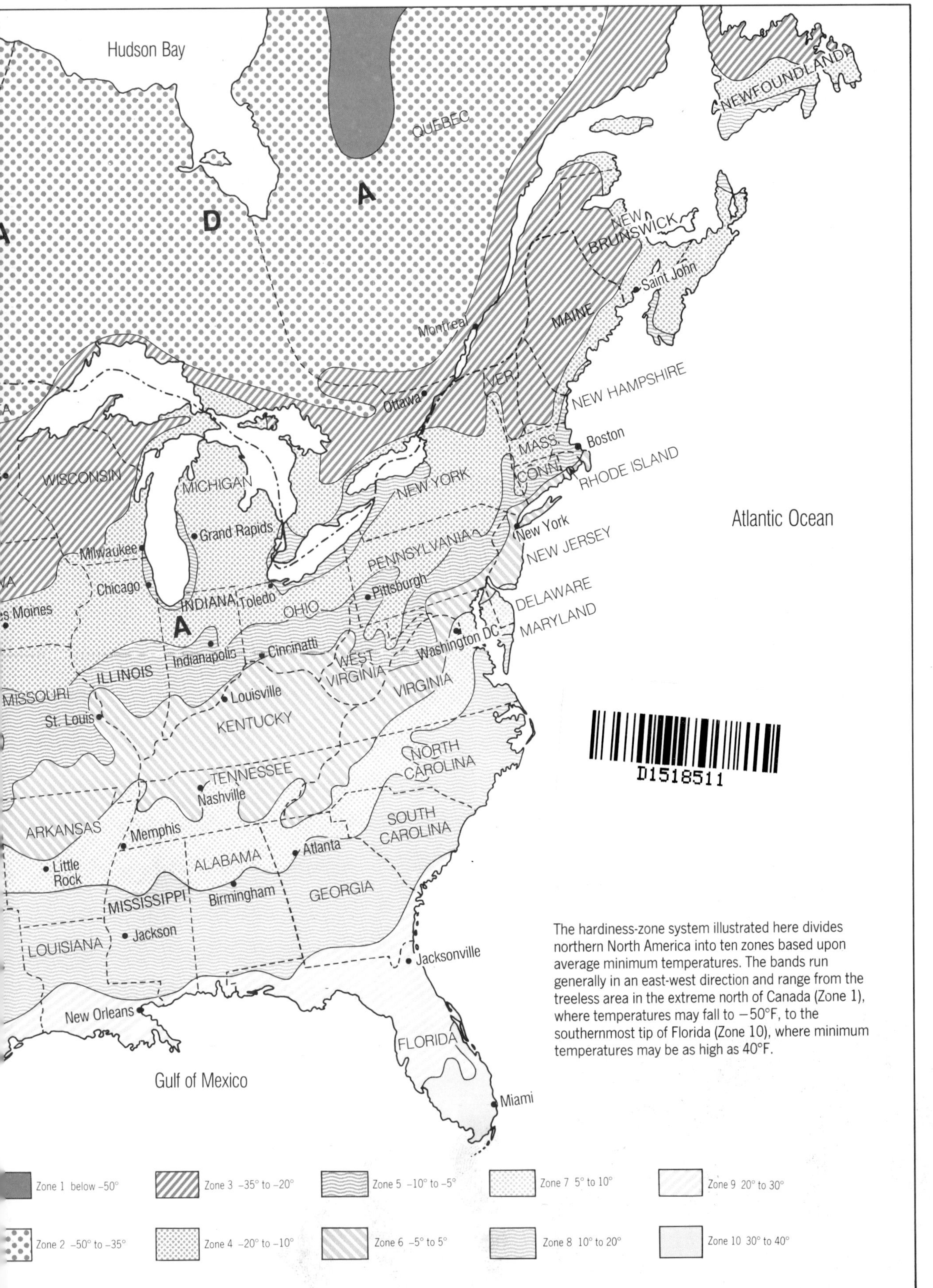

The hardiness-zone system illustrated here divides northern North America into ten zones based upon average minimum temperatures. The bands run generally in an east-west direction and range from the treeless area in the extreme north of Canada (Zone 1), where temperatures may fall to −50°F, to the southernmost tip of Florida (Zone 10), where minimum temperatures may be as high as 40°F.

MAGNOLIAS

This book is dedicated to plant collectors and hybridizers past and present, who collectively have enriched our gardens with a race of plants without equal in the plant kingdom.

Series Editor · Vincent Page

Magnolias

James M. Gardiner

Chester, Connecticut

First American edition published in 1989 by
The Globe Pequot Press, Chester, Connecticut 06412.

Library of Congress Cataloging-in-Publication Data

Gardiner, James (James M.)
Magnolias.

(Classic garden plants series)
Bibliography: p.
Includes index.
1. Magnolia. I. Page, Vincent. II. Title.
III. Series: Classic garden plants.
SB413.M34037 1989 635.9/773114 88–33464
ISBN 0–87106–644–0

Produced by the Justin Knowles Publishing Group,
9 Colleton Crescent, Exeter, Devon, England

Illustrations: David Ashby
Zone map courtesy Swallow Books Ltd

Manufactured in Hong Kong

Contents

List of Photographs

Foreword

Jim Gardiner undertook this work because he knows that great things are happening in the genus *Magnolia*. He feels that the sleeping beauty is awakening at last, and he wants all of us to learn to grow and enjoy these remarkable trees and shrubs. How long has the beauty been asleep? Well, *M. soulangiana* is still about the only clone widely available in nurseries and garden centers in North America, the British Isles, and the continent of Europe, and this primary hybrid was named after one Etienne Soulange-Bodin in the year 1820.

Paleobotanists consider the Magnoliaceae, the family in which magnolias are placed, to be the oldest of all the angiosperms, or flowering plants. In a line of descent not far removed from magnolia, they place the Heath family, including rhododendron. Who ever heard of a gardener who loved and appreciated the one genus and not the other? Both have an evident beauty and aura of 'class'.

The late Dr John M. Fogg, Jr., founder of the American Magnolia Society in 1963 and an insatiable world traveler, always maintained that *M. grandiflora* is the most widely cultivated tree in the world. It flourishes in both torrid and temperate zones wherever sufficient heat, rainfall, and humidity exist. It now grows with such vigor in China, for example, that its seedlings are widely used as understock for propagating native Chinese magnolias.

M. acuminata has an enormous range in the time-worn hills of the eastern and midwestern United States. It even reaches the shores of lakes Erie and Ontario and peeks into southern Canada. An arrow-straight trunk and dense, bright green foliage, combined with great cold-hardiness, make this beautiful tree a standout in any forest. (A tree in North Canton, Ohio, for example, is 95ft (29m) tall and 6ft 6in (2m) in diameter.) The flowers, alas, are small and glaucous blue-green, with inner petals bright yellow. In the southern part of its range, the entire flower is bright yellow. This species has been placed in a different sub-genus (*Yulania*) from the other magnolias in North America. The remaining members of *Yulania* are Asiatic, and all of them will readily cross with their hardy, homespun cousin from the United States.

Grown today as well are vigorous young hybrids of *M. acuminata* and *M. kobus*; *M. liliiflora*; *M. denudata*; *M. sprengeri* 'Diva'; *M. sargentiana* var. *robusta*; and, yes, even the peerless Queen of Magnolias, *M. campbellii* of the Himalayan ranges. Seedlings of the first five crosses have bloomed, bringing exciting new color breaks of bright yellow, pink, peach, and apricot to the magnolia breeders' palette and giving promise, a few decades ahead, of big, luminous, clean pink flowers of *M. campbellii* blooming on tall, straight, and bone-hardy hybrids.

Michelia is another genus with many beautiful but tender species. Some of these have been crossed with *M. acuminata*, so far producing only rather small yellow flowers. Intrageneric hybrids of *Michelia* are also blooming beautifully and with great fragrance in Louisiana.

It is a rare honor indeed to be invited to write this foreword to Jim Gardiner's comprehensive new magnolia book. His deep horticultural background and well-developed taste in classic ornamental trees and shrubs make him an ideal choice to write such a needed work.

Philip J. Savage,
former president,
American Magnolia Society

Introduction

The range of plants that we can use in our gardens is wide; between them the many genera available meet most planting requirements. But it is uncommon to find a single group of plants capable of covering the entire spectrum. The magnolia, however, does exactly that and it is also one of the most beautiful plants available to us today.

One of the most influential of all plant collectors, E. H. 'Chinese' Wilson, wrote of magnolias: 'Aristocrats of ancient lineage possessed of many superlative qualities are the Magnolias. They have the largest flowers and largest individual leaves of any hardy group of trees. No other genus of hardy or half hardy trees and shrubs can boast so many excellences.'

He added, 'Their free flowering character and great beauty of blossom and foliage are equalled by the ease with which they may be cultivated'.

Wilson was right. Magnolias are very variable in habit, from a small shrub to a large tree. Their flowers differ in size, in scent, and in colour, from a pure white through to a rich royal purple. Plants can be seen in flower over a nine-month period, from February onwards. The leaves are either deciduous or evergreen, sometimes with a rich russet-brown indumentum on the underside.

My first real encounter with the richness and diversity of magnolias was as a student gardener in the gardens of the Great Park at Windsor. *Magnolia stellata* 'Water Lily' and Magnolia 'Charles Raffill', that sensational tree magnolia with its large magenta flowers, were my favourites at that time. 'Water Lily' is well suited to all sizes and styles of gardens – in Japan it is sometimes known as the 'Magnolia of the houses', as it can be brought indoors in tubs so that the subtle fragrance of its flowers may be appreciated. At Windsor it snuggled among drifts of dwarf rhododendrons, creating just the right contrast in colour and habit. The Valley Gardens, where the land falls away towards Virginia Water, also make a perfect setting for 'Charles Raffill', which is at its most dramatic seen against the leafless outlines of oak, chestnut, and beech on a still sunny morning in early spring.

The effect must have been rivetting on those plant collectors who first saw these Asiatic tree magnolias flowering in the wild. Frank Kingdon Ward saw *M. campbellii* var. *alba* flowering in the Indian state of Manipur, 'bearing enormous cold moons at the end of its leafless twigs, but with an inner glow as if they might after all be white hot.'

The intimate part of the Hillier Gardens and Arboretum known as Ten Acres is studded with a multitude of magnolias. Walking through this area on a still summer evening yields a variety of scented flowers, each attracting its own pollinators and visitors of the human type. Often out of reach are the big, creamy white, richly scented flowers of *M. hypoleuca*, a forest tree from the island of Hokkaido, Japan. The fragrance of this species is surpassed only by *M.* × *wieseneri*, which combines the intense fragrance of *M. hypoleuca* with the more subtle scents of *M. sieboldii*. If there was a perfume league this would surely win it by its sheer audacity.

Yet scent is not peculiar to mid-summer flowering species; spring and late summer provide us with a diversity. *M. grandiflora*, that elegant evergreen species from America, exudes a soft lemon-citrus scent from its magnificent white flowers, which are surrounded by large, bold, shining, leathery green leaves. The combination of flower and foliage is truly a memorable one. This is nowhere more apparent (apart from in the plant's native country) than on the northern shores of the Mediterranean, where great tree pyramids can be found up to 80ft (24m) high.

I hope this book will stimulate those few gardeners who have yet to discover the charms of magnolias to do so, and that it will encourage those who have already been hooked to seek out more and to grow a wider selection.

The Story of the Magnolia

Henry Compton (1632–1713) was one of the great gardeners of his day. He was also Bishop of London and head of the church for the American Colonies. In this capacity he sent to North America missionaries charged with sending back plants as well as spreading the gospel. One of them was John Bannister (1654–92), who had showed a great interest in botany while an undergraduate at Oxford. In 1678 he arrived at Charles Court County, Virginia, where 'he industriously sought for plants, described them and drew the figures of the rarer species'. In 1688 he sent to Compton the Sweet Bay Magnolia, *Magnolia virginiana*, thus introducing the first magnolia to the British Isles.

M. grandiflora, perhaps the most cultivated of all evergreen ornamental trees, was probably introduced into Britain before 1730. Phillip Miller, in the first edition of *The Gardeners' Dictionary*, published in 1731, wrote:

> There is also another species [apart from *Magnolia virginiana*] which has lately been brought to England. This is esteemed one of the most beautiful trees in America, where they usually grow in moist swampy woods and do often rise to a height of 60 feet or more . . . . Since they are hardy enough to endure the cold of our climate in the open ground, I doubt not but in a few years we shall have the pleasure of seeing its beautiful flowers. . . .

Among the first to grow this plant were the Duchess of Beaufort at Chelsea, Mr Peter Collinson at Peckham, Sir John Colliton at Exmouth, and Sir Charles Wager at Parsons Green (who was the first to flower the species).

Interest quickly shifted to the Asiatic species, which started coming in about fifty years later. *M. denudata* (the Chinese Yulan or Lily Tree) was the first temperate Asiatic species to be introduced by Sir Joseph Banks, in 1789. The third Duke of Portland, in between his prime-ministerial duties, was responsible for the introduction of *M. liliiflora* (the Purple Magnolia) from China in 1790.

The combined resources of these two species resulted in the ubiquitous *M.* × *soulangiana* arriving on the scene, producing its characteristic waxy flowers in a variety of colours. We have Chevalier Etienne Soulange-Bodin, formerly a French cavalry officer, to thank for this splendid hybrid. Sickened by the Napoleonic wars in Europe, he wrote in the *Gardeners' Magazine* of 1819: 'It had doubtless been better for both parties to have stayed at home and planted their cabbages. We are returned there and the rising taste for gardening becomes one of the most agreeable guarantees of the repose of the world.' Soulange-Bodin founded the Royal Institute of Horticulture at Fromont near Paris and became its first director. His most celebrated horticultural deed was to cross *M. denudata* with *M. liliiflora* and to raise this famous group of hybrids from 1820 onwards.

In the transactions of the Linnaean Society of Paris of 1827 we read:

> By the crossing of a Magnolia Yulan (*Magnolia denudata*), grown from seed with the pollen of the Magnolia discolor (*Magnolia liliiflora*), the Fromont Gardens have witnessed the birth, growth and establishment, amongst the varied specimens to be admired there, of a new hybrid which is remarkable for its tree-like habit, its handsome foliage and above all for its widespread brilliant flowers, in which the purest white is tinged with a purplish hue. My worthy colleagues have named this beautiful species *Magnolia soulangiana*.

It was probably around this time that *M.* × *soulangiana* was first introduced to the British Isles, as a description and an illustration drawn from a plant growing at Young's Nursery at Epsom appeared in the Botanical Register for 1828.

It was not until 1852, when Commodore Perry's American squadron opened up Japan to foreign trade, that Japanese plants became available to the Western world. *M. stellata*, the Star Magnolia, reached Britain only in 1877; it flowered a year later at Veitch's Coombe Wood Nursery. A number of attempts had been made to introduce this species prior to this. In the end the successful route was via Rhode Island, New York, where Dr George Hall had been successfully growing the species for 16 years, ever since the winter of 1861.

The Himalayan species, by and large, were not introduced until the early part of the 20th century, when they were sent back by famous plant collectors such as Ernest Wilson, George Forrest, and Frank Kingdon Ward. However, *M. campbellii*, the Queen of Magnolias, was introduced mid-way through the 19th century, probably in 1868. When *M. campbellii* was featured in *Curtis's Botanical Magazine* of 1885, Sir Joseph Hooker recorded that a flower of this species 'was sent from Mr Crawford's well known garden at Lakeville near Cork in 1878', thus making us postulate the earlier introductory date.

The name

Pierre Magnol, after whom the magnolia is named, was a physician and botanist of Montpellier in southern France and an inspired teacher. He had been nominated for the Chair of Botany and the Directorship of the Botanic Garden in 1667, but, because of religious differences, he was not appointed until 1694.

Distribution

Today there are approximately eighty species of magnolia growing in two distinct temperate and tropical regions of the world – eastern America and eastern Asia. The majority are found in eastern Asia, from Manchuria, Korea, and Japan, south through China and the eastern Himalayas to Java and Malacca in the Malaysian archipelago. The American magnolias are found from southern Canada, south through the eastern United States, the West Indies, Mexico, and Central America to southeastern Venezuela.

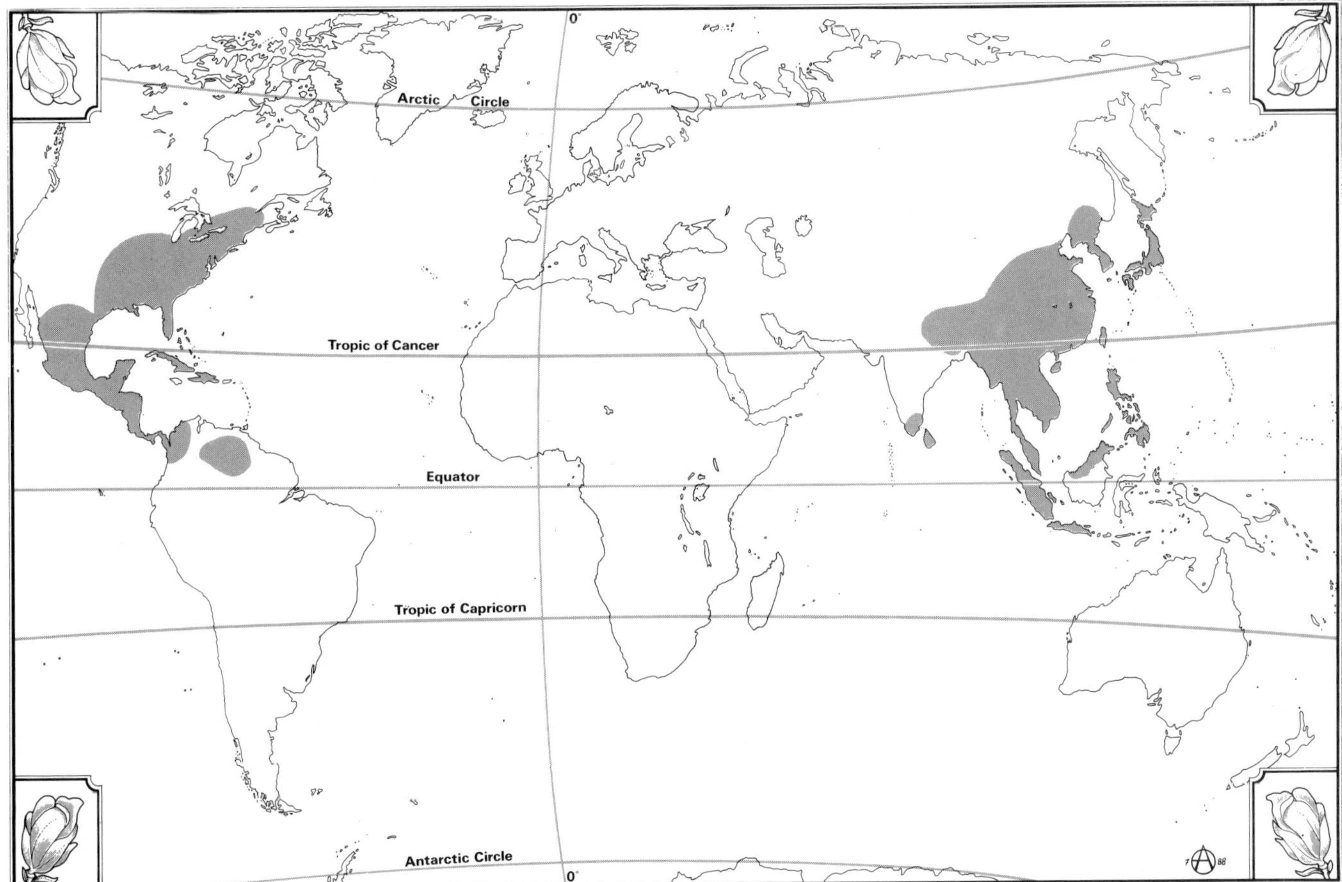

The distribution of Magnolia, Manglietia, and Michelia. The solid black areas show the two quite distinct regions of the world to which these superb plants are native. The majority are found in eastern Asia, from Manchuria, Korea, and Japan, south through China and the eastern Himalayas to the Malaysian archipelago, with outposts in southern India and Ceylon. The American species are found from southern Canada, south through the eastern United States of America, the West Indies, Mexico, and Central America, to Venezuela.

Origins

Magnolias are believed to be some of the most primitive of flowering plants, with evidence of fossil remains being found in rock belonging to the tertiary period (2–65 million years ago). At that time much of the present arctic zone was probably free of ice and enjoying a European climate, typical of the present day. Vast forests encircled the arctic regions with magnolia, liriodendron, liquidambar, gingko, and many others enjoying widespread distributions. Towards the end of the tertiary period a dramatic change in weather conditions occurred with the formation and expansion of the polar ice cap, thus destroying the vast forests found there. Most of the so-called primitive plants were virtually destroyed in Europe, while those of most of China, Japan, and regions of North America were saved. This partially explains why the floras of China, parts of Japan, and eastern North America in particular have similar groups of plants today.

Classification

Magnolia is the largest of eleven closely related genera, the majority being tropical in distribution. Manglietia and Michelia are worth mentioning, as a few species from each genus are grown outside in the British Isles, and Liriodendron, with two hardy species, should also be included.

Magnolias are divided into what are known as sub-genera. This is a botanical term under which a number of species within a genus are grouped together, because they share common characteristics. Magnolias are divided into two groups. Group 1 comprises plants that flower before or at the same time as the leaves; all plants in this group are deciduous. It is known as subgenus Yulania. Group 2 is characterized by the flowers appearing after the leaves; this group contains both deciduous and evergreen species. It is known as subgenus Magnolia. American and Asiatic species can be found in both groups.

Flowers and fruits

The illustration of *M. denudata* (see opposite) shows the structure of magnolia flowers and fruits. G. H. Johnstone, in his *Asiatic Magnolias in Cultivation* (1955), first used the term 'tepal', as most magnolias show no differentiation between petals and sepals. The tepals are arranged in two or more whorls with from three to six in each.

Flowers are protected by perules, which are often furry in those magnolias that flower before the leaves appear. These are shed as the tepals begin to expand, with the flower opening fully within a few days of the perules being shed.

The male part is known as the androecium, which is composed of stamens spirally arranged around the base of the female part or gynoecium. This is a stigmatic column or cone composed of numerous carpels.

Provided that pollination has taken place, the fruit cone turns red or pink on ripening. Once this happens, the fertile carpels split longitudinally, partially revealing the ripened seed, which varies in colour from orange and scarlet to pink according to the species. Seeds are suspended on fine threads, which make it more likely for them to be blown clear of the tree canopy and therefore gives them a better chance of growing away after germination.

Pollination

Magnolias are pollinated by flower beetles, which crawl between the overlapping tepals of an unopened flower. It is important to note that the female stigma is receptive only at this time, therefore it is crucial for beetles to have called on open flowers to become covered in pollen. This is a rich food source for the beetles and consequently they become covered in it. This technique of pollination has remained virtually unaltered since magnolias evolved all those millions of years ago, as none of the more traditional pollinators (bees, wasps, butterflies, moths) had then evolved.

Medicinal Uses

The medicinal qualities of magnolias have been known for centuries in China, the first reference being in the *Cheng Lei Pen Tshao* (Chinese Pharmaceutical Natural History) published originally in 1083. *M. officinalis* (Hou-phu) is a species most commonly cultivated for medicinal use, especially in Szechwan and Hupeh, where the thick bark and flower buds are used. An infusion of the bark yields a cure for coughs and colds and is used as a tonic during convalescence. The flower buds are used for feminine ailments. *M. liliiflora* (Mu-lan) is also recorded in the Pharmaceutical Natural History, where it is reported to be used as a drug plant. *M. denudata* (Hsin Iyu-lan or Yulan), has been used for centuries as a food plant and supplier of medicinal preparations. The tepals are used for food, whilst the bark has medicinal uses for treating colds. A similar preparation made from the bark of *M. kobus* is considered effective by the Ainu in Japan.

Magnolia denudata, *showing the flowers at various stages of development, from bud to blossom, and (bottom left) a fruit cone and its seeds.*

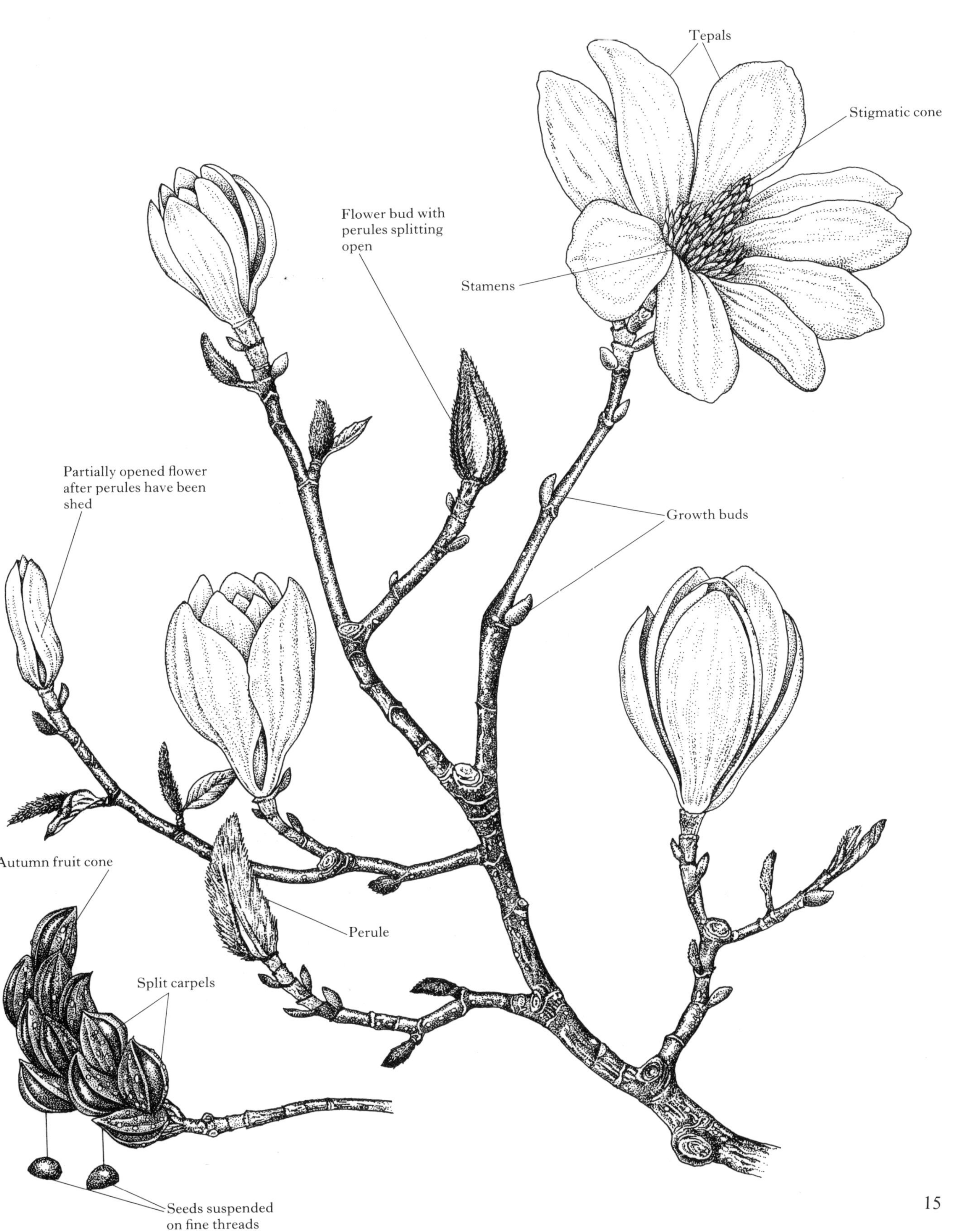
Tepals
Stigmatic cone
Flower bud with
perules splitting
open
Stamens
Partially opened flower
after perules have been
shed
Growth buds
Autumn fruit cone
Perule
Split carpels
Seeds suspended
on fine threads

American species, too, are used in local medicines, with the bark of *M. grandiflora* providing a stimulant, tonic, and drug. The genus Talauma, which is closely related to Magnolia and is restricted to the tropics of Asia and America, also had medicinal value. *Talauma mexicana* was known to the Aztecs as Yolloxochitl, meaning Heart Flower, referring to the shape of the flower buds. It was cultivated in the 15th and 16th centuries for its bark, which was used for a variety of medicines considered effective against fevers, heart diseases, paralysis, and epilepsy.

Economic Uses

The timber from a number of species is used for a variety of purposes. *M. hypoleuca* and *M. kobus*, both Japanese species, have a close-grained, light yellow, soft wood, which is easily worked. *M. hypoleuca* is used for furniture making, utensils, cabinet work, and engraving. North American species are also used. *M. acuminata* and *M. macrophylla* both have soft, durable, close-grained yellow-brown wood. This is widely used for flooring and cabinet work, while *M. virginiana* is sometimes used to manufacture broom handles.

Michelia is closely allied to Magnolia and is restricted to warm, temperate, and tropical Asia. Many species are used locally for their light yet durable timber in houses, furniture, and coffin construction. All the parts of *Michelia champaca* plants seem to have a practical use. In Siam the flowers are used as a cosmetic, and a volatile oil is extracted from them and used in perfumes. The bark is used in a drink with febrifugal properties, while the timber is used extensively for furniture making, door panels, and tea chests. Even the leaves are used – they form a principal source of food for the silk worm.

Liriodendron, another Magnolia ally from eastern North America, has similar wood properties to those already mentioned, but is also the source of Tulipiferine, an alkaloid that acts violently on the heart and nervous system.

Magnolia Art and Folklore

The flowers of *M. denudata* are often pictured on Chinese porcelain, paintings, and tapestries of the Tang dynasty (AD 618–907), because they were regarded as symbols of candour and purity.

One of the first illustrations of a magnolia to appear in Britain was a drawing by Georg D. Ehret of *M. grandiflora* that was published in *The Natural History of Carolina* in 1737. To make the drawing Ehret walked the three miles from Chelsea to Parsons Green to watch the tree, which was in the garden of Sir Charles Wager, open its first blooms. Ehret was regarded as one of the finest botanical artists of his time. He was the son of a Heidelberg market gardener and after a short spell of training as a gardener took up botanical draftsmanship. After spells in Switzerland and France, he moved to England in 1735. At that time, plants were being introduced principally from North America and many wealthy patrons wanted paintings of the new plants they were growing.

The New World is not without its intriguing tales. In the Carolinas, *M. grandiflora* emits a powerful fragrance, which, from a distance, is delicious but when close to is over-powering. The native Indian tribes are said to avoid sleeping under this magnolia when it is in blossom and a single bloom placed in a bedroom is said to cause the death of any person who sleeps there.

Cultivation

Conditions in the Wild

In the chapter on Magnolia Species (page 103), I indicate the type of habitat in which these plants are found growing in their native environments. The understanding of these conditions can be of great benefit to the gardener when choosing a site and deciding which magnolia to plant there – after all, much of the art of gardening lies in reproducing for our plants the conditions in which they will be most comfortable, deceiving them into believeing that they are in their natural habitat.

It is worthwhile recalling some remarks made by people who have seen magnolias growing in the wild in North America and Asia and learning from their observations. Ernest Wilson, who introduced more magnolias into cultivation than any other plant collector, wrote:

> In China and for that matter in Japan and Korea also, Magnolias are found in moist woods growing in association with broadleaved, deciduous trees among which coniferous trees are scattered. They love a cool soil rich in woodland humus.

Euan Cox, plant collector, grower, and author, who accompanied Reginald Farrer to Upper Burma, commented;

> Even in that climate (Hpimaw in Upper Burma) where summer sun is at a premium, all Magnolias seem to prefer company and grow either in medium woodland or on the outskirts of the thick jungle. An odd thing about those Magnolias is we never saw a poor specimen . . . every tree was shapely and every tree was healthy; this was all the more striking in comparison with the general decrepitude around them.

J. Ohwi, in *The Flora of Japan*, pointed out that:

> Magnolias are constituents of the temperate and boreal regions and are found predominantly in mixed deciduous coniferous woodland but can (*Magnolia stellata*) be found on open boggy sites.

T. D. Elias, in *Trees of North America*, noted that all native magnolias grow in moist soils along the margins of streams and ponds and lower mountain slopes. They are seen at their best in deep rich woodlands of the southeast.

Climatic Conditions

Climatic data applicable to our own gardens should now be assessed to see whether it is too hot or cold, too wet or dry, too sunny or cloudy for our proposed magnolia planting plan to take shape. But this is where the difficulties begin, since a whole book on climatic data could be written on the British Isles alone, let alone North America, continental Europe, and all the other countries where magnolias are grown.

The British Isles

Living in the British Isles and having gardened as far apart as Edinburgh in the north, Romsey (Hampshire) in the south, Cambridge in the east, and Liverpool in the west, I should have a good understanding of the British climate. But I know better than to make facile general assumptions. Climatic conditions, like gardening, throw up many interesting surprises. A few years ago I visited the gardens at Howick in Northumberland, not a mile from the northeast coastline of England and about thirty miles due north of Newcastle upon Tyne. Imagine my disbelief when I saw a 35ft (10.5m) *Eucryphia cordifolia* growing, or rather luxuriating, there. For this is a plant that you would normally see in Cornish gardens or in gardens of southwest Scotland or southern Ireland warmed by the Gulf Stream, yet here it was thriving in a garden on the northeast coast of England, in what would seem the most inhospitable of regions, where northeasterly gales have a free passage over the North Sea from Scandinavia and beyond.

The point is that the gardens at Howick have their own microclimate, as do all gardens. Microclimates can also be found *within* gardens, most obviously around the north and south walls of a house, but also in particularly exposed or particularly sheltered planting sites. For instance, during the winter of 1981/82 a minimum temperature recorded at the Hillier Gardens and Arboretum was 3°F (−16°C) on an exposed site, yet not far away in a sheltered site 10°F (−12°C) was recorded (both are within US hardiness zone 7, but at the top and bottom of the zone).

But what climatic conditions suit magnolias in the British Isles? Moisture levels for growth, summer temperatures for ripening of the wood, and winter temperatures for hardiness ratings are points to look out for. It is worth comparing your local climatic readings with those where magnolias are grown. Throughout the book examples of magnolias grown at the Hillier Gardens and Arboretum have been quoted, and for this site the relevant data is as follows:

Average rainfall: 32.5in (83cm) over 168 days
Wettest month: December, 5in (12.2cm)
Driest month: April, $1\frac{1}{2}$in (4.1cm)

Average temperatures
July maximum: 71°F (21.5°C)
July minimum: 53°F (11.5°C)
January maximum: 44°F (6.5°C)
January minimum: 34°F (1°C)
Daily maximum (1986): 88°F (31°C)
Daily minimum (1986): 13°F (−10.8°C)

Magnolias are grown extensively in several countries. Highlighted below are climatic readings from areas where magnolias are cultivated successfully.

North America

North American weather patterns are enormously complex, with tremendous variations occurring. Before looking at specific areas in North America where magnolias are cultivated, mention should be made of a chart giving North American hardiness zones which has been prepared by the United States Department of Agriculture and the Arnold Arboretum. There are ten zones, with each zone equating to a minimum winter temperature banding. Zone 1, for example, equates to temperatures below −50°F (−45°C) (areas of northern Canada). Zone 8 has temperatures ranging between 20°F (−7°C) to 10°F (−12°C) (parts of Oregon, California, Georgia, North Carolina), similar in fact to most of the British Isles. Zone 10 equates with 30°F (−1°C) to 40°F (5°C) (Los Angeles, San Francisco, and southern Florida).

The northwest coastal regions are nearest to the British climate, with their summers being similar to those of the southeast of England. Winters are usually mild, not falling below 10°F (−12°C), although the winter of 1972 saw temperatures plummet to as low as −19°F (−28°C).

The San Francisco Bay area has low rainfall – 22in (55cm) spread over 67 days. The wettest month is January, with $4\frac{3}{4}$in (12cm), and the driest are July and August, with less than $\frac{1}{10}$in (2.5mm). Coastal fog keeps summer temperatures down, with 65°F (18°C) and 53°F (11.7°C) being the maximum and minimum average temperatures for July. The winter temperatures are mild, with 55°F (13°C) and 45°F (7°C) being the maximum and minimum averages for January. Frosts have been known to occur.

The Gulf region is variable. It is hot and dry inland, but on the coast at Mobile 62in (157cm) of rain falls on 120 days. August is the wettest month, with $6\frac{3}{4}$in (17.3cm) falling and October is the driest with $3\frac{1}{2}$in (8.9cm). The high temperatures reflect the steaming southern atmosphere, with 90°F (32°C) and 73°F (23°C) being the average maximum and minimum temperatures for July and 60°F (15.6°C) and 44°F (6.7°C) being those for January.

A number of famous magnolia collections are found in Michigan, yet it has the reputation of not being a particular friendly environment. The total annual rainfall is $32\frac{1}{2}$in (81cm) on 137 days, June is the wettest month, with $3\frac{1}{2}$in (9.1cm), and January and February share the distinction of being the driest, with 2in (5.3cm). The state's unfriendly reputation is because of its low winter temperatures, with 31°F (−0.8°C) and 19°F (−7.2°C) being the average maximum and minimum temperatures for January. There is, however, a complete turnaround in Michigan in midsummer, specifically in July, with 82°F (28°C) and 63°F (17°C) being the average maximum and minimum temperatures for that month.

The northeast coast around Boston has grown and still does grow fine magnolia collections. Boston's yearly rainfall is 41in (104cm) on 125 days, with a fairly even distribution – $3\frac{3}{4}$in (9.6cm) in March, the wettest month, and 3in (7.8cm) in May, the driest. There is, though, a wide variation in temperature, July's average maximum and minimum being 80°F (26.7°C) and 63°F (17.2°C) while January's are 36°F (2.2°C) and 20°F (−6.7°C).

Continental Europe
Holland is probably more famous for its production of magnolias than for its collections. However, the Von Gimborn Arboretum allied to the University of Utrecht has a fine collection. Rainfall in the coastal belt of Holland is 28½in (72cm) per year on 186 days, November with 3⅓in (8.3cm) and March with 1½in (3.5cm) being the wettest and driest months respectively. The July average maximum and minimum temperatures are 70°F (21°C) and 58°F (14.4°C), while the January averages are similar to those of the southeast coast of England, being 41°F (5°C) and 33°F (0.6°C).

Rainfall figures for the area around Lugano in southeast Switzerland are 68in (172cm) per year on 118 days, with October having 7¾in (19.8cm) and January and February having 2½in (6cm). Average July maximum and minimum temperatures for July are 83°F (28.3°C) and 60°F (15.6°C) – high enough for good summer ripening. The January maximum and minimum temperatures are 43°F (6.1°C) and 29°F (–1.7°C).

Magnolias are cultivated with great enthusiasm in southern Scandinavia where summer temperatures are not often high enough to ripen wood in preparation for the winter onslaught. Yearly average rainfall (including snow) in the southeast of Sweden is 29in (75cm) with rain and snowfall averaging 2in/2in (5cm/5cm) split in January and rain averaging 3in (7..5cm) in July. Average temperatures for January are 17.6°F (–8°C) and for July –10°F (15°C).

Japan
Japan's native magnolias are spread over most of the islands, with the Island of Hokkaido growing the hardier forms. Sapporo has 41in (104cm) of rain per year on 138 days, with a maximum of 5in (12.7cm) falling in September and only 2¼in (5.5cm) falling in April. High summer temperatures of 75°F (24°C) and 58°F (14.5°C) are the maximum and minimum temperatures for July. These are followed by low winter temperatures, with January's averages being 29°F (–1.7°C) and 11°F (–11.7°C) – figures which reveal why only the hardy forms of magnolias are found here. Tokyo, in eastern central Honshu, is wetter and hotter, having 61½in (156cm) of rain each year on 107 days, with September, the wettest month, having 9¼in (23cm) and January, the driest, having 2in (4.8cm). July temperature averages are 83°F (28°C) and 70°F (21°C) while January's are 47°F (8.3°C) and 29°F (–1.7°C).

New Zealand
The North Island has an excellent reputation for growing magnolias, particularly in the areas around New Plymouth on the southwest coast. Annual rainfall is 60½in (153cm) on 188 days, with July, the wettest month, having 6¼in (16cm) and March, the driest, 3½in (9.1cm). The average maximum and minimum temperatures are 70°F (21°C) and 55°F (12.8°C) for January and 55°F (12.8°C) and 43°F (6.1°C) for July.

Hardiness, Shelter, and Shade
The question is often asked, is the plant hardy? More often than not a straight yes or no is given without further qualification. But what is meant by hardiness and why do plants from the same genus or even the same species react in different ways?

When magnolias are introduced into areas of the world that are outside their natural distribution, they have to adjust to new climatic conditions. This is often a severe test. How successfully a plant meets the challenge depends on the degree of natural hardiness that it has developed through the evolutionary process and also the level of temperature drop to which it is accustomed in its home habitat. For instance, *M. grandiflora* in its natural geographic range can experience minimum temperatures between 43°F (6°C) and 10.4°F (−12°C), dependent on location. However, when introduced into an alien environment it is often expected to grow in conditions where temperatures can drop to −0.4°F (−18°C).

A plant's ability to withstand low temperatures can also often depend on its geographic origin, its age, and its health. What then are the environmental factors that affect our plants' performance?

Cold Damage

Cold damage may be best considered under two main headings: (a) winter injury when the plants are relatively dormant, and (b) autumn or spring injury when there is some active growth.

The climate in which a magnolia grows in the wild is usually a good guide as to its relative hardiness. However, there are always one or two surprises – *M. delavayi*, for example, is proving more resilient than was first expected. Plants from northerly latitudes, such as *M. acuminata* and *M. tripetala* from the New World and *M. kobus*, *M. hypoleuca*, *M. stellata*, and *M. sieboldii* from the Old, are proving to be the most hardy. It is those magnolias from southern locations, especially evergreens, that are vulnerable to winter injury, with *M. grandiflora*, *M. nitida*, and *M. globosa* (the Chinese form) proving particularly susceptible. Clonal differences and differences between species will show clearly here, with some plants coping while others suffer from dieback, defoliation, or death. Age and the physiological condition of the plant can also effect its chances of survival, with young plants (under approximately seven years) and plants whose growth rate is generally poor being more susceptible to freezing conditions. (It is worth mentioning here that containerized magnolias are particularly susceptible to frost damage).

It is root systems that are killed during periods of severe winter weather, so it is the roots that should be given protection. Although evergreens can take up water when temperatures are as low as 28°F (−2°C), a combination of biting winds and frozen ground is particularly damaging, then the foliage becomes dehydrated also.

Autumn injury is noticed with some of the North American deciduous species. *M. macrophylla* in particular continues growing late into the season and consequently suffers from dieback when frost affects the soft shoots.

Spring injury is probably the most damaging, not to the survival of the plant itself but to its flowers. In maritime climates, wintry conditions often return after cold spells during December or January, when buds have already started to swell. This can have disastrous consequences. The entire flower crop may be frosted, with the tepals 'browned' completely or just at the margins, or bleached of their colour. Early-flowering varieties, such as *M. campbellii* and its close relatives and *M. kobus*, are particularly susceptible.

Plant breeders give considerable thought to improving the hardiness ratings of plants by selecting specific clones or by taking a species known to be very hardy and hybridizing it with another species not famous for this quality. In the de Vos and Kosar hybrids, for example, *M. stellata* improves the hardiness of *M. liliiflora* 'Nigra'.

Heat

Heat does not appear to trouble magnolias unless it is a dry heat coupled with dry soil conditions. A number of species and hybrids have been planted widely in the tropics without adverse effect. However, some growers believe that deciduous plants need low temperatures at certain times of the year, otherwise their flower development will be adversely affected. On the other hand, magnolias need adequate summer temperatures to ensure shoot growth and ripening. If this shoot ripening does not take place, plants that are normally tolerant of low winter temperatures will suffer from shoot dieback or even death.

Shelter

In the wild most magnolias are plants that like companionship. In other words, they are found growing in close association with other plants. This is because they are not pioneer plants and to be successful they need a gradual build up of leaf litter and humus around them to provide their roots with a soil rich in nutrients. They also require a soil that is shaded by a leaf canopy so that it does not heat up and dry out too quickly.

We can reproduce these conditions artificially by feeding and mulching around the base of the plant so that it can be 'isolated' as a lawn specimen. The need to mulch and keep the roots shaded grows less as moisture levels, i.e. rainfall and atmospheric humidity, increase. This is why magnolias can and are grown quite successfully in urban areas with comparatively few signs of vegetation around. Isolation, though, means that the plant loses the shelter of a crowd of companions.

October 1987 saw hurricane force winds batter the southeast corner of England. Many magnolias were lost because other trees fell on them, others had branches ripped off, but most came through unscathed – a telling demonstration of how the magnolia's pliancy gives it the ability to withstand such winds.

However, some species do demand some degree of wind filtration. Despite being surprisingly hardy, the American species *M. macrophylla* indicates by the size of its foliage a need for some shelter, although it does adapt to more exposed positions by producing smaller foliage.

When planting a new garden, consider traditional wind breaks such as birch, larch, alder, holly, or pine, or even the ubiquitous Leyland Cypress, to give instant shelter to magnolias. If there is no room for these traditional shelter plants, try some of the smaller magnolias, which are more tolerant of exposure.

Shade

Certain magnolia species under certain climatic conditions will be grateful to be given some shade. As a rule of thumb, the hotter and drier it is, the greater the need for shade. In most places in the British Isles it is unnecessary to provide shade – the majority of magnolias will simply enjoy any sun on offer. Of the exceptions, *M. wilsonii*, *M. sinensis*, *M. sieboldii* (and its hybrids), and *M. globosa* need shade where the summers are hot and dry, but will be quite happy in full sun where moisture and humidity levels are high. In certain instances the light levels are not good enough for successful cultivation. The Pickard hybrids are very successful in the high light areas of Kent and central and southern Europe but in more northerly latitudes their flowering is not nearly so spectacular.

PROPAGATION

Magnolias can be successfully propagated in a number of different ways – from seed, by cuttings (which may be of either softwood or semi-ripe wood), by layering, by chip budding, and by grafting. Only the first three of these methods are likely to be employed by the amateur gardener.

Seed

The advantages of raising magnolias from seed are as follows:

1 It is a means of introducing new cultivars through either controlled or uncontrolled hybridization.
2 It widens the gene pool, if seed is collected from native habitats.
3 It is cheaper than raising plants by vegetative means.
4 It generally gives fast establishment and good growth.
5 It produces vigorous root systems, which is particularly beneficial when seedlings are used as understocks.
6 Seed can easily be moved from one country to another.
7 Considerable genetical variation is found in seed collected from a cultivated source where open pollination has taken place.

A disadvantage is that seed-raised plants generally take longer to flower than vegetatively-raised plants, though many of the recent American hybrids raised from seed are flowering in under ten years.

There is a wide variation in the availability of seed from species grown in the British Isles. The very-early-flowering species, like *Magnolia campbellii*, do not set seed primarily because of low temperatures and lack of pollinators at the time of flowering. Late flowerers, like *M. grandiflora*, do not fruit because temperatures are generally too low also at the other end of the season, during the autumn. A number of species, such as *M. cylindrica*, do, however, seed prolifically.

Ripening of the fruiting cones can take three or four weeks in the British Isles, by which time seeds can be seen when the fruiting-cone carpels split open, normally in October. It is important that the fruiting cones are left on the plant until this time as it is difficult to extract the seed any earlier. Once this stage is reached, the fruiting cones can be collected, dried, and the seed shaken free.

Do not overdry to the point where the coat becomes shrivelled, as the viability of the seed will then be impaired. The coat's bright colouring attracts mammals and birds, who assist with the seed's dispersal. Being oily and sticky, it also waterproofs the seed and forms a protective covering that prevents germination as long as it remains intact.

The seed should be cleaned by soaking in warm or hot water to which a detergent has been added to remove any remaining traces of the oily film. Seed can be sown either in the autumn or in the spring. This ultimately depends on the scale of operation and the facilities available.

The following method can be employed for small-scale production with limited facilities. Sow the seeds thinly in a seed tray or similar container filled with a soil-less seed compost. Lightly cover the seed with compost followed by approximately $\frac{1}{4}$in (6mm) depth to $\frac{1}{8}$in (3mm) of grit. (The addition of grit has the advantage of considerably reducing the amount of moss or liverwort that will grow on the surface of the compost.) Water. Place the labelled and dated seed tray in a cold frame where the seed will be exposed to low temperatures. This will remove any germination inhibitors prior to the seeds germinating in the warmth of spring. As this system is not 'controlled', germination of some seed may be delayed for a season, so retain your seed tray for a further 12 months.

The second system is far more controlled. In fact a timetable could be prepared to determine when you store, when you sow, and when to expect germination. Seed is mixed with moist peat or peat and sand/vermiculite and stored in labelled polythene bags in a refrigerator at a temperature held between 34°F (1°C) and 37°F (3°C) for two months. (Forty-two days has in fact been shown to be sufficient.) The addition of a five-per-cent fungicidal solution to the stratification medium will help reduce the incidence of damping off diseases at the germination stage. At this stage the seed can be sown in a similar way to that mentioned above and placed in a temperature of 70°F (21°C). Germination can be expected within 30 to 40 days of placing in the higher temperature.

Seedlings are then pricked out into individual 3$\frac{1}{2}$in (9cm) pots into a well-drained soil-less compost incorporating a slow-release fertilizer.

Cuttings

The main advantages of raising magnolias from cuttings are as follows: 1 An exact copy of the parent plant is produced. 2 Plants will flower from an earlier age (as compared with seed-raised plants).

The main disadvantages are: 1 Cuttings are more costly to produce. 2 They are less easily carried from country to country, because of import/export restrictions.

A wide range of magnolias can be propagated by cuttings.

There are essentially two types of cuttings, based on the stage of stem development, namely: 1 Softwood cuttings (deciduous species and cultivars). 2 Semi-ripe cuttings (evergreen species and cultivars).

Softwood Cuttings

The cuttings are removed at the junction of the current season's growth with the previous year's hardwood. The material is taken when the base of the cutting has become firm. The time at which this occurs is dependent on a number of factors which mainly revolve around whether the parent plants have been forced into growth under glass or polythene or are growing in the garden. Growth responses vary from species to species or cultivar to cultivar. This also affects the time at which cuttings are taken, as does the geographical location of the source of the cutting material.

Where container plants are kept under glass or polythene, sun heat alone will induce early shoot growth which can firm sufficiently in early May for cuttings of 3–5in (7.5–13cm) in length, dependent on species or cultivar, to be taken (see the illustration below). The growing tip is generally removed, which induces quicker rooting. Wounding is also beneficial and can be either light or heavy dependent on the plant being rooted (*M. stellata* would have a light wound, whereas the thicker stemmed *M.* × *soulangiana* would have a heavy wound). This increases the quantity and quality of the roots as well as increasing water uptake by the cutting prior to rooting. With large-leaved subjects (*M.* × *soulangiana*) approximately half of the leaf blade is removed, which reduces water loss and increases the number of cuttings inserted into a given area. If this is done fungicidal treatment is most important as disease is more likely to occur because of the increase in the number of cut surfaces on the cutting.

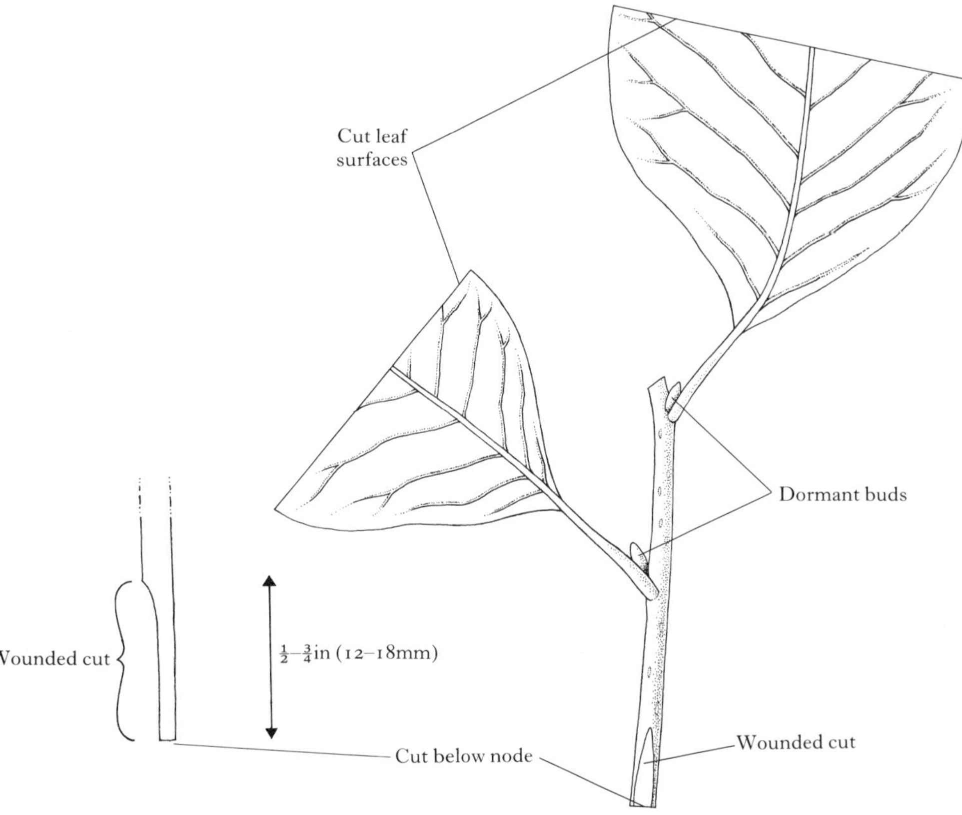

A softwood cutting, illustrated on Magnolia × soulangiana, *showing the wounding of the stem and the removal of approximately half of the leaf blades. The cutting is about 5in (13.5cm) long. The side view of the bottom of the cutting shows a detail of the wounded cut itself.*

The application of hormone rooting powder is most effective, with up to a 90 per cent take being expected; 0.5 per cent IBA (Indole butyric acid) in talc for thin-stemmed subjects such as *M. stellata* and 0.8 per cent IBA in talc for *M.* × *soulangiana* is recommended.

The key to success in rooting softwood cuttings is to take cuttings from plants which are in a healthy condition. Plants which are in a poor state of health, either through age or growing conditions, generally take far longer to root (if they root at all) than do strong, vigorous plants. Cuttings should be kept turgid from the time of collection until they are rooted. They can be rooted in a variety of protected structures: cold frames, mist-progagation units, closed cases, fogging systems. However it is the aftercare which is of vital importance if these cuttings are to root.

The optimum rooting-medium temperature is 65°F (18°C) to 70°F (21°C) with air temperatures around 70°F (31°C). The cuttings should be shaded by reducing the light levels by approximately 25 per cent of average summer light conditions. Always check for fungal problems each day.

Rooting media can vary from nursery to nursery. Two parts peat and one part sharp sand or perlite is probably the most commonly used, or alternatively pine bark (cambark fine grade), peat, and perlite in equal proportions or just bark and peat in equal proportions can be used. It is also desirable to add a controlled-release fertilizer such as Osmocote (6 to 9 months) to maintain nutrient levels in the cutting and the compost and improve rooting performance.

Cuttings are inserted into trays, cellular trays, or individual pots, the advantage of the last two over trays being minimal root disturbance. Rooting takes place in about eight weeks and it is most important for the survival of the cutting over the first winter that shoot growth is initiated as soon as possible. Do not disturb the cuttings until they have just started into growth in the following spring. In many instances apparently healthy cuttings fail to grow away the following year – the reason for this is obscure but it is thought to have to do with nutrient balance within the plant.

Semi-ripe Cuttings

Evergreen species and cultivars can be propagated successfully by semi-ripe cuttings taken during late August or early September in southern England. *M. grandiflora* and *M. delavayi* can both be propagated successfully this way.

Nodal cuttings 5in (13.5cm) long, with a heavy wound and their leaf blades reduced, are inserted into cellular trays or individual pots after being dipped in 0.8 per cent IBA in talc.

Similar protected structures, temperature regimes, and rooting media as for soft wood cuttings are used here.

Rooted cuttings remain in trays over the winter months and are potted up in the spring. If cuttings are inserted later in the autumn (October) they will generally callus in the autumn and root in February for potting in March or early April.

Layering

This has long been a standard method of plant raising for deciduous magnolias or where a small number of plants is required. Layering differs from other propagation methods in that it involves the development of adventitious roots on a stem which is still attached to the parent plant. Prior to layering, thoroughly cultivate the soil and work in liberal quantities of peat and sharp sand. During March, layer the shoots of the previous season's growth and make a tongue by cutting along the length of stem as illustrated opposite. This technique is particularly useful because, although magnolia stems are reasonably pliable they tend to be brittle when bent to this degree. Dust the cut sliver with 0.8 per cent IBA in talc. Peg the layer firmly in the ground and tie up the stem with a cane.

The tongue cut into the stem of the parent plant should be about 2in (5cm) long. Bend the stem carefully at the tongue cut and peg it firmly into the ground, tying the stem to a cane. The bend in the stem at the tongue cut should be approximately 3in (7.5cm) below the level of the soil. When the layer is well rooted, cut the stem as indicated.

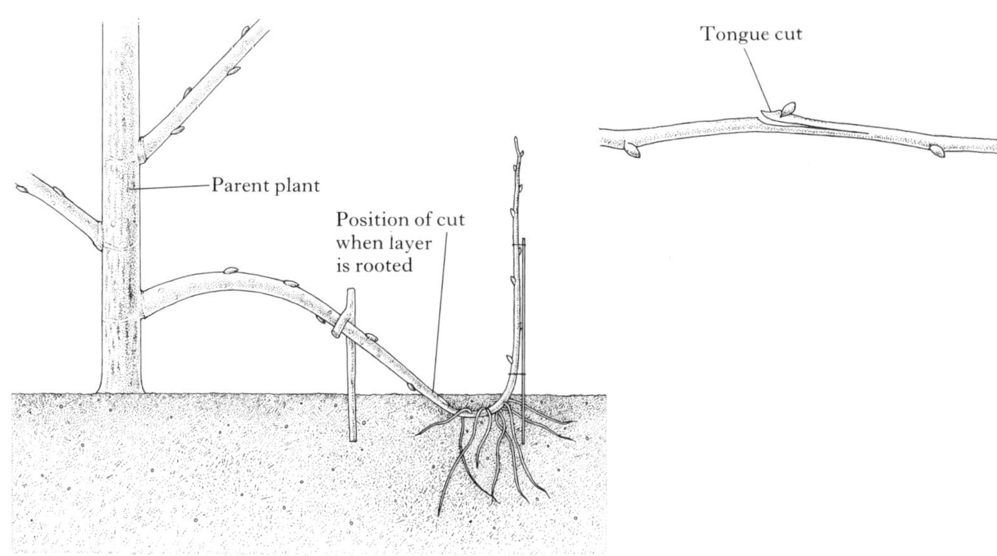

Examine the layers after 12 months and if they are well rooted completely sever them from the mother plant. The root layer can then be lifted and containerized in October (18 months from time of layering). Alternatively it can be left until the following March or April (that is to say, until 24 months after layering) and then containerized.

Chip Budding

Chip budding has been recognized as a way of propagating open-ground trees since the 1930s, but it was not until David Knuckey presented a paper on his experiences with T and chip budding of magnolias on to pot-grown seedling root stocks that magnolia propagation moved forward.

Chip budding is the substitution of the scion, consisting of a bud, rind, and sliver of wood, for a matching area of root-stock tissue. Stocks are seedling raised and potted up individually into 3in (7.5cm) square pots and are generally ready for budding 18 months after germination. The stocks are fairly closely (botanically) matched with the scions being budded. The table on page 28 lists many magnolias that may be used as scions and shows stocks with which they may be matched.

The following is the procedure that has been used successfully by Hillier Nurseries (Winchester) Ltd. Stocks are lined out in a greenhouse controlled at a temperature of 60°F (15.5°C). Scion wood is collected in July.

A chip bud (see illustrations, page 29, top row) is married up with the stock and held in place by means of a 1in (2.5cm) wide clear polythene strip, making sure that the dormant bud on the scion is not covered over (see illustration, page 29, centre).

Bud takes are recognized quickly with the bud swelling and the leaf petiole abscissing clearly within ten days. The stock is cut back to just above the bud to promote the channelling of all the growth into the developing shoot. By the end of October a shoot 3in (7.5cm) to 4in (10cm) in length will have been produced (see illustration, page 29, bottom left) which then goes dormant. During this time the polythene strip is left on and the budded plants remain in a cool greenhouse at 48°F (8°C).

The three-month period from budding to dormancy is crucial to allow for sufficient

Scion	Stock
M. cordata *M. cylindrica* (*M. kobus*, *M.* × *loebneri*, *M.* × *proctoriana*, *M.* × *salicifolia* and varieties, and 'Wada's Memory' can also be budded but are generally propagated by cuttings)	*M. kobus*
M. campbellii and varieties *M. campbellii* var. *mollicomata* and varieties *M. denudata* *M. dawsoniana* *M.* 'Chyverton' *M. sargentiana* var. *robusta* *M. sprengeri* 'Diva' (also cuttings) *M. sprengeri* var. *elongata* (also cuttings) *M.* 'Albatross' *M.* 'Caerhays Belle' *M.* 'Charles Raffill' *M.* 'Eric Savill' Gresham hybrids (also cuttings) *M.* 'Iolanthe' *M.* 'Mark Jury' *M.* 'Michael Rosse' *M.* 'Princess Margaret' *M.* × *veitchii* (also cuttings)	*M. campbellii* var. *mollicomata* or *M. sargentiana* var. *robusta* or *M.* × *soulangiana* if no other stocks are available
M. dealbata *M. fraseri* *M. macrophylla* *M. macrophylla* subsp. *ashei* *M. officinalis* *M. officinalis* var. *biloba* *M. tripetala* *M.* × *wieseneri* *M.* 'Charles Coates' *M.* 'Silver Parasol'	*M. hypoleuca* or *M. tripetala*
M. globosa *M. sinensis* *M. sieboldii* *M. wilsonii*	*M. sinensis* or *M. sieboldii*

Chip budding, illustrated on Magnolia × wieseneri. *The bud stick should be about 6in (15cm) long, the chip bud should be about 1¼in (3cm) long, and the leaf petiole about 1in (2.5cm) long (far right). Attach the chip bud to the root stock with a clear polythene tie, about 1in (2.5cm) wide (centre). It is essential that the polythene does not cover the bud, or it will impede growth, but it must hold the chip bud firmly in place so that the connection between scion and stock is closely made. The top growth on the root stock should be retained to encourage the flow of sap.*

scion growth to take place. This ensures that the shoot breaks into growth the following spring and grows away successfully.

The following spring, successfully budded plants are potted into 7in (18cm) pots into a peat, bark, and grit compost with a slow-release fertilizer added. Rapid growth follows which can produce a plant of 5ft (150cm) in 15 months from budding and leaves the marriage of scion and stock looking as shown on page 29, bottom right.

The Saratoga Horticultural Foundation in California has developed a successful technique to T bud selected forms of *M. grandiflora* on to seedling root stocks during April with a single stem plant ready for sale within six months.

The chip bud three months after preparation and insertion, seen from the side (right) and front (far right)

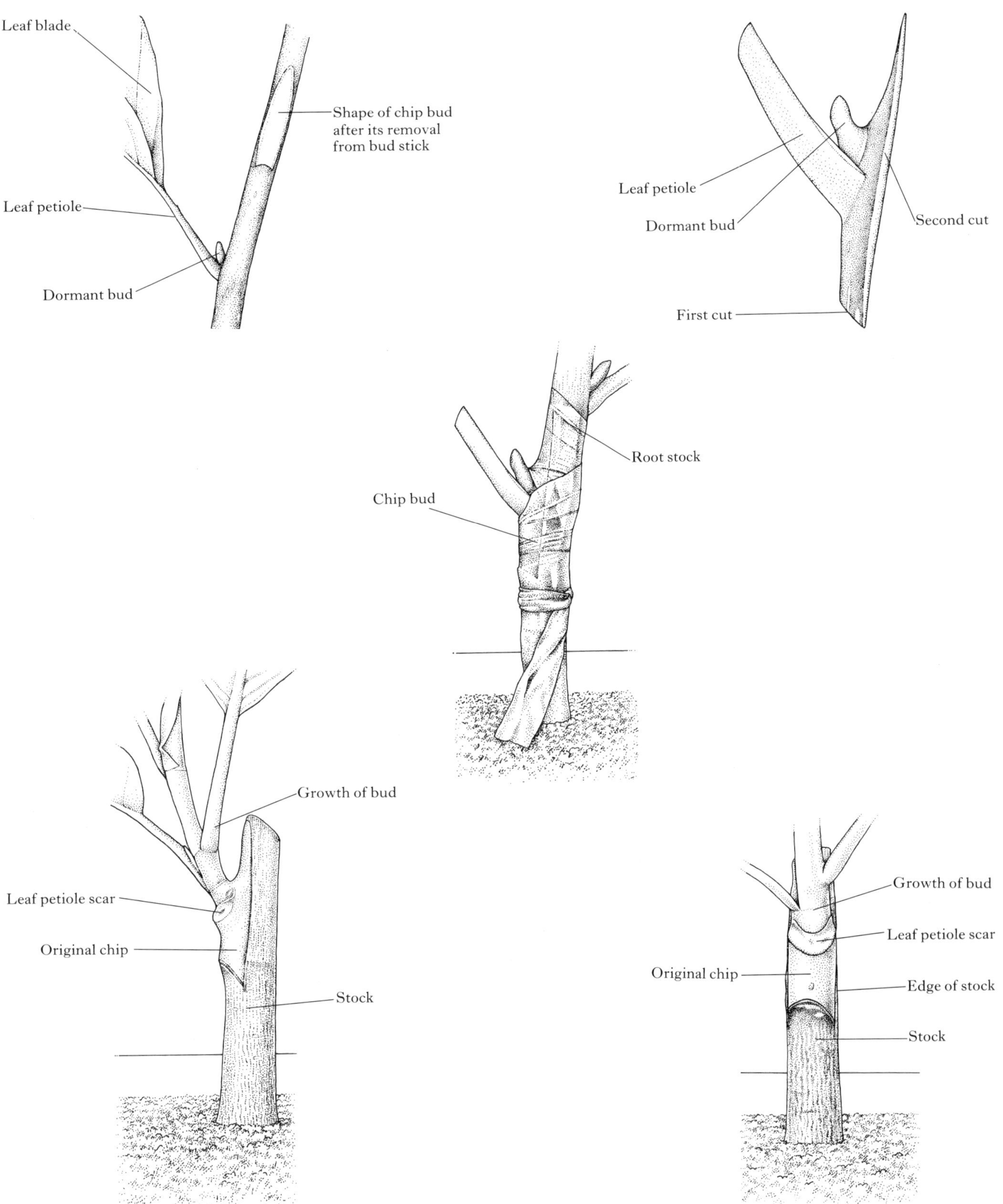
Leaf blade
Shape of chip bud after its removal from bud stick
Leaf petiole
Dormant bud
Leaf petiole
Dormant bud
Second cut
First cut
Root stock
Chip bud
Growth of bud
Leaf petiole scar
Original chip
Stock
Growth of bud
Leaf petiole scar
Original chip
Edge of stock
Stock

Grafting

Bench grafting has largely been superseded by budding as the latter technique enjoys the advantages that: 1 It is economic of scion wood. 2 It has a high overall percentage take. 3 It produces a more uniform plant. 4 It requires less skill.

Where grafting is practised, it is carried out between mid-August and March, depending on the variety and how it fits in with nursery working practices. Similar subjects are grafted to those that are budded.

Winter Grafting

Stocks are brought into growth during late January, some three weeks before scions are collected. A side veneer graft is the best method here, with the union taking place close to the roots of the stock plant. The stock and scion are bound together with a rubber grafting tie. The stock plant is headed back but sufficient growth above the union is maintained to 'pull' sap upwards. This is then placed in a high-humidity tent in a temperature of approximately 60°F (15.5°C).

The plants will slowly grow away over the next two-month period. More air is given to harden off the grafts gradually. The stock can now be headed back to just above the union. An unsightly graft union often produces a poorly growing plant in later years unless scion rooting occurs.

Summer Grafting

This is usually carried out towards the end of July. The stocks are dealt with by removing any side shoots or leaves which would interfere with the graft. Half the number of leaves are left on the scion, which is prepared, tied, and placed in a high-humidity tent and shaded from direct sunlight. The ties used and techniques employed are similar to those used in winter grafting. Successful grafts are gradually hardened off and maintained in a greenhouse over winter and are potted up the following spring.

PESTS AND DISEASES

Magnolias are comparatively free from attack by any of the usual garden pests and they suffer less than most shrubs from disease. Like any other plants, however, they ask to be grown under healthy and appropriate conditions – not, for example, in frost pockets or water-logged soils – if they are to live a long, problem-free life. Granted that, they are unlikely to cause their growers much anxiety. The few pests and diseases that might be troublesome can be dealt with in a mercifully short chapter.

Pests

Slugs

Slugs feed at night and are particularly active during warm humid evenings. Young magnolias are particularly vulnerable to slug attack during the first year of planting. If the slugs are left unchecked they can virtually defoliate the plants. In subsequent years, when the plants are established, comparatively light damage is done. There are a number of control measures available, the majority of which can only be used on a small scale. However, a solution of potassium permanganate and aluminium and copper sulphate can be watered into the soil around the plant to control slugs for several months. Pellets containing methiocarb are effective for a few days only when scattered in the vicinity of the plants, but young children and cats should be kept away from treated areas.

Other 'safe' control measures include sinking shallow dishes containing beer to soil level, or trapping slugs by laying old cabbage leaves, grapefruit skins, etc within the vicinity of the plant to be protected.

Red Spider Mite

Magnolias being grown under glass or polythene are susceptible to infestations of red spider mite. These can be particularly severe between July and September if left unchecked.

Provided no other spray programmes for other pests take place within the greenhouse complex, a natural predator can be introduced to control the mites. If this introduced early enough in the season it may, together with high temperatures, succeed in keeping the spider mite at bay. A range of chemicals is also available; these should be rotated at frequent intervals to reduce the risk of resistance. Derris is a particularly safe chemical to use.

Scale
Magnolia scale and Liriodendron scale are serious pests of magnolias in the United States. A spray of dormant oil, such as Scalecide or Volck, in early spring is nontoxic and very effective.

Diseases

Cankers
Stem cankers attributed to Phomopsis are occasionally found. Canker on cuttings in mist benches has been blamed on *Phomopsis syringae* (Lilac blight) but it occurs so infrequently that it is not a problem.

Magnolia leaf spot (Phyllosticta magnoliae)
Irregular spotting on leaves, especially of *M. grandiflora*, occurs, especially in warm humid climates. It is not considered to be a problem.

Honey Fungus (Armillariella mellea)
This is a very common fungal disease in gardens today; it affects a wide range of woody plants and is especially prevalent in wet areas. It is a secondary infectant entering plants that are in stress because of old age, drought, waterlogging, frost cracks in the bark or damage caused by tools or lawnmowers.

Magnolias are highly resistant to this disease. I have come across only two plants that had succumbed to the fungus. When it does strike, the plant's vigour is considerably impaired; the leaves become smaller and often look chlorotic. Large specimens decline over a number of years. There is no cure. Complete removal of the stump is essential.

Verticillium Wilt Diseases
Although there appears to be no record of this disease affecting magnolias in the British Isles, there are several recorded cases of *Verticillium albo-atrum* affecting magnolias in North America. Apart from the brown/black discolorations which run in the conducting elements, the distinguishing feature of this disease is that sections of the crown or even complete sides of the tree die quite suddenly. Verticillium wilt is very difficult to tackle in this situation. However if the affected specimen is very small, a soil drench of the benomyl at fortnightly intervals during the time of the collapse is worth considering.

Magnolia virus
Mottled line patterns, rings, and oak-leaf patterns are occasionally seen on magnolias. They are thought to be caused by the cucumber mosaic virus.

MAGNOLIA × SOULANGIANA Chevalier Etienne Soulange-Bodin was responsible for introducing this most celebrated of all magnolias into horticulture, by transferring pollen from *Magnolia liliiflora* on to *M. denudata*. This resulted in a number of seedlings being produced from 1820 onwards and over the years selected forms from similar breeding lines have been named in Europe, America, and Japan.

RUSTICA RUBRA
A vigorous plant of spreading habit producing a rich display of rose-purple goblets during late April, this selection, raised at Boskoop, Holland, in 1893, is reported to be a chance seedling of *Magnolia* × *soulangiana* 'Lennei'.

PICTURE
This hybrid (above) was found in 1930 in the garden of Kaga Castle in Japan by Koichiro Wada, a Japanese nurseryman, who propagated two plants. Several years later plants of this spectacular *Magnolia* × *soulangiana* hybrid arrived in the United Kingdom.

ALBA SUPERBA
One of the best of the white-flowering forms, 'Alba Superba' (right) has a hint of purple at the base of the tepals. Slightly scented, it is one of the first *Magnolia* × *soulangiana* hybrids to bloom. It was raised by Van Houtte in Ghent, Belgium, in 1867.

MAGNOLIA × SOULANGIANA
A group of magnolias, mainly *Magnolia × soulangiana* selections, growing at the United States National Arboretum in Washington, D.C. The vast majority of *soulangiana* selections form large, spreading shrubs or small trees. Flowers vary in colour from pure white to rich purple, but all have the classic goblet shape.

LENNEI ALBA
'Lennei Alba' (left) is an ivory-flowered third-generation seedling from *Magnolia × soulangiana* 'Lennei' that was raised by Froebel of Zurich, Switzerland, in 1905.

MAGNOLIAS IN PHILADELPHIA
A splendid group of magnolias (below), including *Magnolia × soulangiana*, part of the collection at the University of Pennsylvania's Morris Arboretum in Philadelphia.

LENNEI
Magnolia × soulangiana 'Lennei' (above) probably arose in Italy in the late 1830s. A distinctive seedling was bought by a Prussian nurseryman, who named it in honour of Peter Lenne, the then Superintendent of the Prussian Royal Gardens.

SAN JOSE
This *Magnolia × soulangiana* hybrid (right) was raised by the San Jose Nursery Company of California and introduced in 1940. Its flowers are creamy white, heavily flushed with pink on the outside. It is pictured here at the Henry F. Dupont Garden in Delaware.

TOM DODD SEEDLING #4
'Tom Dodd seedling #4' is a *Magnolia × soulangiana* seedling that was sent to the United States National Arboretum in Washington, D.C., by the Tom Dodd nursery of Mobile, Alabama, for evaluation.

MAGNOLIA CAMPBELLII VAR. ALBA
Magnolia campbellii var. *alba*, here (left) growing wild at Dochu La in Bhutan, was introduced into the United Kingdom by the late J. C. Williams of Caerhays Castle in the southwest of England.

MAGNOLIA CAMPBELLII
This, the 'Queen of Magnolias' (right), was discovered in Sikkim in southeast Asia by Sir Joseph Hooker, who, in 1885, named it after Dr Archibald Campbell.

MAGNOLIA CAMPBELLII VAR. ALBA

The flowers of *Magnolia campbellii* var. *alba*, here (right) growing in the gardens of Wakehurst Place in southeast England, are large white 'moons', produced on the plants after 14 or 15 years.

MAGNOLIA CAMPBELLII
The great beauty of this large deciduous tree species is displayed in early spring, when enormous rosy buds burst open, revealing 'sumptuous water lilies poised on leafless branches'.

PRINCESS MARGARET
A pink-flowered seedling of *Magnolia campbellii* var. *alba*, 'Princess Margaret' (left) was exhibited at the Royal Horticultural Society's Show in London in 1973 as 'Windsor Belle'. It received its present name only a few hours later – given the princess's name because of the beauty of its flower.

MAGNOLIA CAMPBELLII VAR. MOLLICOMATA
This large deciduous tree is the eastern form of *Magnolia campbellii*. It comes into flower (right) at less than half the age of *M. campbellii* – at 10 to 14 years – and flowers later in the season, thus missing many spring frosts.

KEW'S SURPRISE
Magnolia campbellii 'Kew's Surprise' was sent to Caerhays Castle in the southwest of England as a numbered seedling in the autumn of 1948. Not being thought particularly promising, it was given a difficult site, close to some large beech trees, when it was planted in 1951. When it eventually flowered it created a sensation with its large cup-and-saucer flowers.

UNNAMED RAFFILL HYBRID
This spectacular *Magnolia campbellii* hybrid (above) is growing in one of England's great gardens, Nymans in West Sussex.

IN WINDSOR GREAT PARK
A selection of unnamed *Magnolia campbellii* seedlings (left) growing in the Valley Gardens at Windsor, in an English landscape fitting in both scale and setting for these magnificent trees.

LANARTH
This sensational form of *Magnolia campbellii* var. *mollicomata* (above) was discovered in the Chinese province of Yunnan and introduced into cultivation by the Scottish plant collector George Forrest in 1924. 'Lanarth', named after the garden in which it was planted, was one of only three seedlings that were raised. The original plant was very vigorous, but its descendants have been grafted on to less energetic root stocks.

SPECTRUM
Magnolia 'Spectrum' (right) is a *Magnolia liliiflora* 'Nigra' × *M. sprengeri* 'Diva' cultivar raised and named by the United States National Arboretum, Washington, D.C. It is a large spreading shrub or small tree that flowers within five years of raising and is hardy to US zone 5.

MAGNOLIA SARGENTIANA VAR. ROBUSTA
This exotic-looking, but quite hardy, tree (left) first flowered in the United Kingdom in April 1931 – with spectacular effect. Its spreading branches bowed under the weight of its giant flowers, which seemed to one observer 'like open parachutes of coloured paper'.

MAGNOLIA DAWSONIANA
This Chinese species (left) was named after Jackson T. Dawson, the first superintendent of the Arnold Arboretum, Boston, Massachusetts. It flowers later than other spring-flowering tree species and is therefore less likely to be damaged by frosts.

MULTIPETALA
A seedling of *Magnolia sargentiana* var. *robusta*, 'Multipetala' (right) was found growing in the Irish garden of Mount Congreve.

ERIC SAVILL
'Eric Savill' (opposite, top right) is an English-raised seedling of *Magnolia sprengeri* 'Diva'. It is seen (right) growing in the gardens of Windsor Great Park, where it was raised.

MAGNOLIA SPRENGERI
When Ernest Wilson saw this species (below) in the woods of western Hupeh in central China, he wrongly believed it to be the wild type of *Magnolia denudata.* It was in fact *M. sprengeri*, a species named in 1912 from material collected by P. C. Silvestri, an Italian missionary, which has 12 tepals against *denudata*'s 9.

CLARET CUP
A *Magnolia sprengeri* bought in 1913 flowered at Caerhays Castle in southwest England for the first time in 1925. So beautiful were its flowers that the variety was later named 'Diva', 'the goddess'. 'Claret Cup' (below right), which is a seedling of that original plant, was grown at Bodnant in north Wales.

MAGNOLIA TRIPETALA
This deciduous eastern North American species (left) is grown in Britain for its large ovate leaves, which are produced towards the end of the shoots in clusters whose shape gives *M. tripetala* its common name of the Umbrella Tree.

MAGNOLIA DEALBATA
In 1570 Philip II of Spain dispatched his physician, Francisco Hernandez, on a scientific expedition to Mexico. The results were published in 1651 under the title *Nova Plantarum Historia Mexicanum.* This work included the first scientific drawing of a magnolia; it was *Magnolia dealbata* (left), the only deciduous magnolia growing in the tropics. It was another 300 years, though, before the species was introduced into cultivation.

MAGNOLIA HYPOLEUCA
This deciduous Japanese species (above) has beautifully scented, creamy white flowers which, during June and early July, fill the surrounding air with 'the rich smell of ripe water melons'. It is one of the hardiest of the tree species.

MAGNOLIA MACROPHYLLA
The Big Leaf Magnolia (right) lives up to its name. The huge leaves are particularly eyecatching when a gentle breeze blows, exposing their greyish undersides.

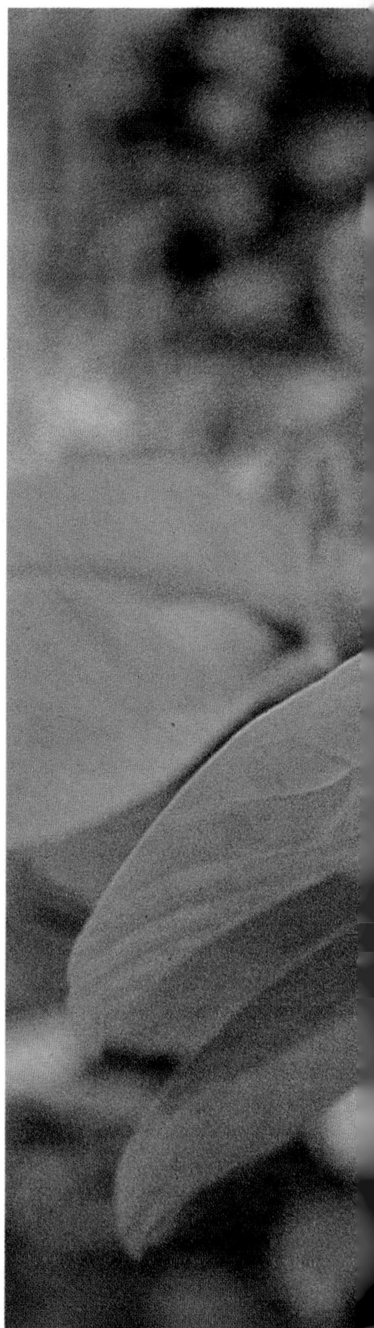

NIGRA
Magnolia liliiflora comes from central China, but 'Nigra' (left), a popular, darker-flowered form, was found by John Gould Veitch in Japan in 1861. It is one of the best of the summer-flowering magnolias and is especially suitable for the small garden because of its compact, rounded habit of growth.

MAGNOLIA CORDATA
This summer-flowering species (above) from the southeastern United States of America is valued for its canary-yellow flowers, although the effect of this unusual colour is diminished because the flowers appear at the same time as the leaves. Some American authorities regard it as a sub-species of *Magnolia acuminata* and refer to it as *M. a.* var. *subcordata.*

MAGNOLIA GRANDIFLORA
Magnolia grandiflora (left) is native to the southeastern United States of America, but has become one of the most commonly grown evergreen trees throughout the temperate world. It is an adaptable species, flourishing in a wide range of climates, and is equally at home freestanding or grown against a wall – as (above) in gardens in southeast England.

MAGNOLIA DELAVAYI
Ernest Wilson introduced this imposing evergreen species (right) from Yunnan in China in 1899. The dull green leaves are some of the largest among evergreen plants. Like *Magnolia grandiflora*, *M. delavayi* is an adaptable plant that is equally happy to be freestanding in a deep, rich soil or against a wall in shallow, chalky soil.

FREEMAN
The *Magnolia grandiflora* for the small garden, this American hybrid was raised in 1930 by Oliver Freeman, who crossed *M. grandiflora* with *M. virginiana*.

MAGNOLIA CYLINDRICA
This aristocratic, white-flowered species (far right, and, above, growing in Windsor Great Park in England) was introduced from eastern China in 1927. Its branches spread horizontally, so that when in flower it looks like a giant candelabra. It takes its species name from the shape of its bright red fruits (right).

PURPLE EYE
'Purple Eye' (above) is thought by some to be a hybrid between *Magnolia denudata* and *M.* × *soulangiana*, but is probably a *M. denudata* clone. It is more vigorous than the type species, with larger leaves and flowers that open later and more widely.

MAGNOLIA DENUDATA
The Yulan, *Magnolia denudata*, has been widely cultivated for centuries by the Chinese and was probably introduced into Japan around a thousand years ago. By the time Sir Joseph Banks introduced it into the United Kingdom in 1789 it must have been hybridized over the years by both the Chinese and the Japanese, so what we see today is almost certainly of hybrid origin. It is quite hardy and is noted for its slow rate of growth and its longevity.

MAGNOLIA DENUDATA
The Yulan (above and right) is one of the most conspicuous of plants in flower, with its slender-necked goblets gleaming in the spring sunshine.

ELIZABETH
During the 1950s Eva Maria Sperber, of the Brooklyn Botanic Garden, crossed *Magnolia acuminata* with *M. denudata.* Years later, in the late 1970s, the resulting hybrid (left) was named 'Elizabeth', after the then director of the Botanic Garden, Elizabeth Scholz. The reason for this belated interest was that 'Elizabeth' bore a fragrant, clear yellow flower on leafless stems – something that hybridizers had long been striving to attain.

ANN ROSSE
Magnolia 'Ann Rosse' (above), with its white, pink-flushed flowers, resulted as a chance seedling of *Magnolia denudata* with *M. sargentiana* var. *robusta*, which is considered to be the pollen parent. It was first raised in the gardens of the Countess of Rosse at Nymans in England.

MAGNOLIA STELLATA
The Star Magnolia (left) is one of the most popular magnolias; it is a multi-branched plant that flowers prolifically. Its compact habit makes it well adapted to exposed sites and it is tolerant of a wide range of soil types.

ROYAL STAR
A vigorous American selection raised in 1947, *Magnolia stellata* 'Royal Star' (below) is extremely cold-resistant, surviving cheerfully temperatures of −29°F (−34°C) in eastern North America.

WATER LILY
A number of distinct forms, with both pink and white flowers, are recorded under this name, but the *Magnolia stellata* 'Water Lily' (above) grown widely in the British Isles is one of Japanese origin. It was distributed by Kluis Nursery of Boskoop, Holland, and introduced into Britain by Hillier Nurseries of Winchester.

ROSEA
Magnolia stellata 'Rosea' (left) is a Japanese selection introduced in 1890. It is valued – and was given its name – for its blush-pink tepals. This feature is more noticeable in older plants, but even then the flowers fade to white as they age.

ROSEA KING
An American selection with pale pink flowers, *Magnolia stellata* 'Rosea King' differs from 'Rosea' (previous page) in having a larger number of tepals and in being more floriferous.

LEONARD MESSEL
Max Loebner, then the Gardens Inspector at the Botanic Gardens of Bonn, Germany, was the first person to hybridize, in 1917, *Magnolia kobus* with *M. stellata* and so to produce an interesting family of free-flowering hybrids that quickly develop into large multi-branched shrubs or small trees. The *M.* × *loebneri* selection shown here (left and, in close-up, below) is named after the late Colonel Leonard Messel, in whose gardens at Nymans in southeast England it originated. It was a chance seedling resulting from *M. kobus* being crossed with *M. stellata* 'Rosea'.

MERRILL
Magnolia × loebneri 'Merrill' (above) is an American selection, raised in 1939 at the Arnold Arboretum, Boston, Massachusetts, and named after a former director of the Arboretum, Dr E. D. Merrill. It is a particularly vigorous variety, upright in habit but spreading with age.

MAGNOLIA KOBUS
This is a common plant in forests throughout Japan; in the wild it varies in habit from a small, round-headed tree to a large pyramid-shaped tree. Trees in cultivation seldom attain a height of more than 40ft (12m) and they are often as broad as they are tall. They are remarkably tolerant of a wide range of soil types, balking only at thin, dry soils over chalk.

KEWENSIS
A free-flowering deciduous hybrid between *Magnolia kobus* and *M. salicifolia*, Magnolia 'Kewensis' (left and below left) bears white flowers which appear on the leafless shoots even when the plants are only a few years old. They have a faint orange-blossom fragrance.

WADA'S MEMORY
Magnolia 'Wada's Memory' produces one of the most spectacular flowering displays of any small tree – the size, quality, and sheer number of the blooms is quite exceptional.

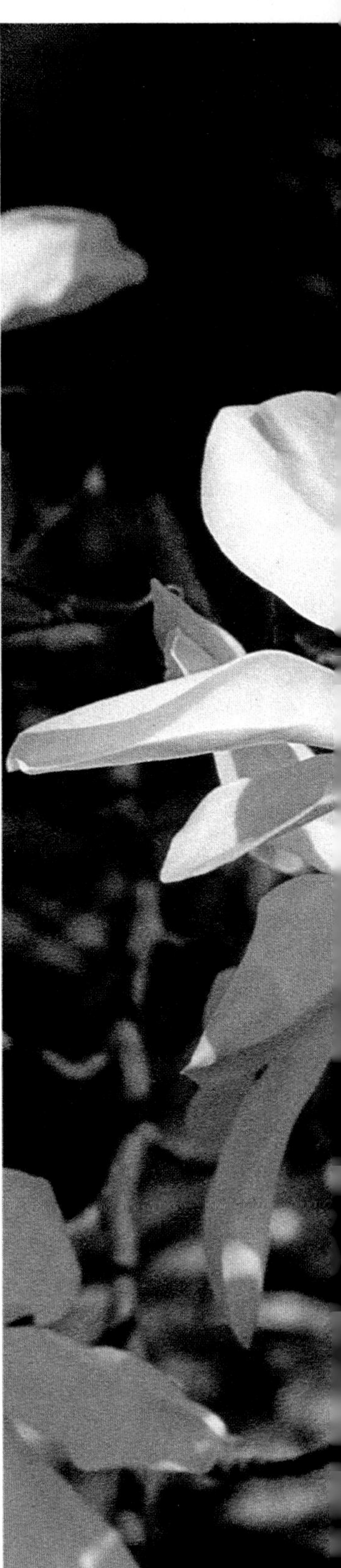

MAGNOLIA × PROCTORIANA Many successful magnolia hybrids have relied on the sharp eyes of a skilled cultivator to notice differences in apparently similar seedlings. This was the case when seed from *Magnolia salicifolia* was sown at the Arnold Arboretum in Boston, Massachusetts. One of the resulting seedlings was seen to bear multi-tepalled flowers like those of *M. stellata.* The discovery was named *M.* × *proctoriana.* It is a small, many-branched tree (above) that bears heavy crops of faintly fragrant flowers (right) on bare stems in spring.

MAGNOLIA SALICIFOLIA
One of the most distinctive features of this, the Japanese Willow Leaf Magnolia, is the lemon-verbena scent given off by the leaves and young shoots when they are rubbed between the fingers. So powerful is the aroma that Ernest Wilson, when he first saw *Magnolia salicifolia* in the wild, 'took this Magnolia for some member of the Camphor family'.

MAGNOLIA SINENSIS
This (above) is a delightful Chinese species with fragrant, saucer-shaped pendent flowers. Young plants grow away strongly and are best trained on a single stem before being allowed to spread their framework of branches. Then the viewer can come close and look up into the beautiful flowers to see them at their best.

MAGNOLIA WILSONII
This Chinese species (left), named in honour of Ernest Wilson, who introduced this and five other magnolias into cultivation, bears fragrant, cup-shaped flowers. It is best trained initially on a single stem like *Magnolia sinensis* – and for the same reason.

MAGNOLIA SIEBOLDII
Among the several desirable features of this aristocratic species (above) are the stiffly held flowers, which are a stunning colour combination of pure white tepals and crimson stamens and are deliciously fragrant.

CHARLES COATES
This (left) is an interesting hybrid between the asiatic *Magnolia sieboldii* and the American *M. tripetala.* C. F. Coates was the propagator in charge of the Arboretum Nursery at Kew Gardens in London, and in 1946 he spotted it as a self-sown seedling growing in the azalea garden. When it flowered for the first time, in 1958, its parentage was established. Being a hybrid it was named after the finder and raiser of its seedling.

MAGNOLIA × WIESENERI
Magnolia × wieseneri (right) is a superbly scented hybrid of Japanese origin which combines the delights of *M. hypoleuca* with those of *M. sieboldii.* Writers have summoned a number of adjectives in attempts to describe its scent, with 'spicy' and 'aromatic' among the most common.

ISCA

In 1907 the British nurseryman Peter Veitch transferred pollen from *Magnolia denudata* on to a good pink-flowered form of *M. campbellii*. Six seedlings resulted, all of which flowered within 15 years. *M.* × *veitchii* 'Isca' (above) is a white-flowered form that was selected from these seedlings.

PETER VEITCH
Magnolia × *veitchii* 'Peter Veitch' (right), named after its hybridizer, is the pink-flowered sibling of 'Isca' and is encountered more often. It flowers prolifically – one 30-year-old tree in the south of England regularly carries as many as 800 blooms on its 60ft (18m) frame.

HEAVEN SCENT
One of the Gresham hybrids, Magnolia 'Heaven Scent' (opposite, top and bottom left) is a selection from the *Magnolia liliiflora* × *M.* × *veitchii* 'Rubra' cross that gives chalice-shaped flowers up to 5in (12.5cm) in length during early and mid-May.

ROYAL CROWN
One of the original Svelte Brunettes raised by Todd Gresham, Magnolia 'Royal Crown' (opposite, bottom right) is similar in parentage to 'Heaven Scent'. The dark red flowers are $5\frac{1}{2}$in (14cm) long.

SAYONARA
Another Gresham hybrid, Magnolia 'Sayonara' (above) is a selection from *Magnolia* × *soulangiana* 'Lennei Alba' × *M.* × *veitchii* 'Rubra' that gives white flowers flushed with a delicate pink at the base of the tepals.

DE VOS AND KOSAR HYBRIDS
During 1955 and 1956 Dr Francis de Vos and William F. Kosar of the United States National Arboretum in Washington, D.C., crossed *Magnolia liliiflora* 'Nigra' with *M. stellata* 'Rosea' to produce this group of fragrant, free-flowering, multi-tepalled hybrids. 'Susan' (above and top right) has deep pink flowers with six uniformly coloured tepals opening to between 4in (10cm) and 6in (15cm) across. 'Randy' (centre right) is a particularly floriferous hybrid with up to eleven spreading tepals, red-pink in bud, opening white inside. 'Pinkie' (bottom right) is probably the most distinctive of the eight de Vos and Kosar hybrids; it has broad, soft pink tepals.

ANN
'Ann' (right) is the earliest-flowering cultivar among the de Vos and Kosar group of hybrids; it has red-pink tepals that remain erect.

MICHELIA FIGO
Michelia figo, the Port Wine Magnolia or Banana Shrub, is native to the warm regions of China and was introduced into Britain in 1789. Although not a shrub of great beauty in flower, it is highly regarded because of its powerful, fruity scent, likened by some writers to that of peardrops.

MAGNOLIAS IN THE GARDEN

Siting: Magnolias in the Landscape

The magnolia is undoubtedly one of the most glamorous and effective of all woody plants for gardens of all sizes. Magnolias are equally effective on the grand scale or in a small suburban garden. In a larger garden, tree magnolias are particularly effective set against a dark background of evergreen plants, when they visually dominate the landscape with their glowing white or rich pink blooms. If your garden is undulating, take care not to plant in a frost pocket. This, in the majority of cases, means that you are forever looking skyward to witness this riot of colour, but that is far better than finding the blooms bleached of their colour because of frosting. It can be a positive advantage to view from below *Magnolia wilsonii*, M. *sinensis*, *M. globosa*, and *M. sieboldii*, with their pendant or nodding flowers. Otherwise, if your garden is large and steeply sloping, you may be able to plant below a terrace or below a convenient viewpoint on high ground so that you can 'stand in the crown' and soak up the overwhelming display of flower power.

Lawns

Lawn specimens can be particularly effective. The archetypal *M.* × *soulangiana* is very useful in medium-to-large gardens, but there is a magnolia to suit most garden sizes. Lawn specimens normally do well, because a covering of grass means no root disturbance, so essential in the cultivation of this genus. However it is important to feed the ground around the plant with a proprietary turf fertilizer (lime free) each spring and autumn; this will reach through to supply the magnolia with a balanced feed. Lawn-planted magnolias, will almost certainly have to be pruned at some time. Information on techniques can be found on pages 101–2.

Containers

The Japanese are particularly fond of containerizing *M. stellata* and its cultivars so that they can bring it into their homes to appreciate its delicate fragrance when in flower. The de Vos and Kosar hybrids can be treated in a similar fashion. From my experience, considerable expertise is needed to retain magnolias in a container for any length of time. The roots are particularly sensitive to being hot and dry during the summer months and frosted during the winter months. However, if these difficulties can be resolved, then the experience of seeing a well grown specimen of the 'Magnolia of the houses' in a conservatory during flowering time can be particularly satisfying.

Mixed Borders

Many magnolias will find themselves in mixed borders with shrubs, herbaceous plants, and bulbs for company. Care must be taken that the plants chosen do not need constant soil cultivation at their bases. Magnolias dislike soil being disturbed around their roots.

Walls

Many a country-house wall would look naked had a *M. grandiflora* not been planted against it. Sites of similar size and scale are not too readily available today. However, slow-growing clones of *M. grandiflora* or less-vigorous hybrids are now available for more limited spaces. Early-flowering deciduous species have also been planted against walls. North walls are to be preferred – they heat up more slowly and do not force the plant into too early bloom so that the flowers run the risk of damage from severe frosts.

Plant Selection

From the outset you should consider what you want of your magnolias. Are you simply growing for aesthetic appeal or are you planting a collection of species and cultivars that are true to name? Either way, you still want to know how your plant is going to grow and whether it is going to perform the function it was selected for.

Most of the reputable suppliers of magnolias will be raising plants vegetatively by cuttings, grafting, or budding. However, a number will still be raising species by seed. If these have been collected and brought back from their native countries that is fine, as no hybridization will have taken place. However, with seed-raised plants from cultivated collections there will be doubt about their authenticity. There are arguments both for and against this technique. Undoubtedly, a number of very interesting and desirable hybrids have been introduced in this way (for example, *Magnolia* 'Charles Coates'). However, against this is the fact that there are a number of poor forms of species in circulation today and only particular clones should be sought (the Korean form of *M. sieboldii* is the most horticulturally desirable form of this species). The only instance where seed-raised plants can be grown from cultivated sources is where flowers have been hand pollinated.

The majority of magnolias purchased today are containerized plants. Pay particular attention to the root systems by examining whether the plant is well established in the container, but not over established with the root system growing out of the bottom of the pot. Many of the deciduous tree species are either budded or grafted (see pages 27–30). Better plants (a better union between the stock and the scion) are obtained when plants are budded. However, this does not preclude the purchase of a grafted plant, provided the scion is vigorous and it is sturdily held in the pot.

Autumn planting is to be recommended. The soil is warm and the roots will continue to grow for a short time after planting. However, the plant should have been hardened off by the nursery beforehand – if it has just come out of a greenhouse or a polythene tunnel, growth will be far too soft and considerable dieback will take place during the winter months. Best results are obtained from spring planting, from March to the end of April dependent on site and situation, provided that container plants are protected from frost during the winter months. Where magnolias have been standing out at plant centres during severe winters they start to break out into growth in the spring and then collapse. This is because the root system has been killed by severe chilling while in the containers. However, if a plant is purchased in the autumn and for one reason or another it cannot be planted until the spring, heel in the plant still in its pot in a protected site until you are ready to plant.

Summer planting from a container is possible provided that you are not in the middle of a drought. Always water freely if there is no significant rain after a week.

Bare-root plants are sold from some suppliers and generally arrive at the beginning of the winter. At no time allow the root system to dry out. Care should be taken when containerizing and with the subsequent after care, as damaged roots are likely to rot during the dominant period. The smallest possible container should be chosen and the compost must be moist but not wet. Once the plant is established in the spring, it can either be potted up for planting the following autumn or directly planted out in early summer, provided that it is large and vigorous enough and that irrigation is available.

Soil Preparation

It is axiomatic that magnolias benefit from thorough ground preparation prior to planting, but how much preparation is needed depends upon the existing state of the soil. The object of the exercise is to produce a rich, fertile loam that is moisture retentive and on the acid side of neutral. If you are fortunate enough to have this 'perfect' soil already, then nothing needs to be done. If, as is more likely, you have not, then you should incorporate liberal amounts of well-rotted bulky organic matter into the soil. This adds 'body' to sandy or thin soils and opens up heavy soils and is imperative if success is to be achieved. With clay soils, it is important to incorporate grit along with the organic matter.

What is the best type of organic matter to use? This depends upon where you live and what is available to you. Acid peat, well-rotted animal manure (horse manure being the best), leaf mould (which is rich in nitrates), conifer needles, shredded bark, coarse sawdust, and chopped bracken are all suitable. However care should be taken before items such as bark or sawdust are used. These should be stacked long enough for their natural toxins to be neutralized and for the damaging nitrites contained in them to be converted by bacterial action into useful nitrates.

Whether planting in sandy or heavy soil, a large planting pit is always to be recommended. For a lawn specimen the ground should be cultivated to two spits deep and a planting pit 4ft (1.2m) across at the very minimum should be dug. If this preparation is being carried out immediately prior to planting, the soil should be broken up into a fine tilth. However, if a planting pit is being prepared in the autumn for spring planting, it should be left as open as possible (especially with heavy clay soils) to allow weathering to take place.

There is a clear distinction between a moisture-retentive soil and waterlogged soil. Magnolias are not swamp plants and therefore, if your heavy soil is rather too moisture retentive, it will be worthwhile draining the site prior to planting. When preparing a planting pit where the clay content of the soil is high, always 'rough up' the vertical sides by penetrating them with a garden fork or a similar piece of equipment. If smooth sides are left the roots will often have great difficulty penetrating them; they will be able to make use only of soil in the dug pit and this will drastically reduce the rate of growth of the plant in the future.

pH

The term used to define the acidity or alkalinity of the soil is pH; pH 7 is neutral, numbers below 7 indicate acidity, numbers above 7 indicate alkalinity.

This is a contentious issue amongst magnolia growers. All agree that an acidic soil is suitable for cultivation, with 5.5 to 6.8 being considered the most desirable range. But some accept that many magnolias can be grown successfully in an alkaline soil. Certainly plants growing on thin soils over chalk or limestone do not flourish, but this may be because these soils heat up quickly in the spring and dry out precisely when water is called for. Most successful magnolia collections are growing where the annual rainfall exceeds 28in (81cm) and where a more-or-less even precipitation occurs throughout the growing season. Some magnolias (*M. grandiflora* and other evergreen species) are more tolerant of drought than others; these are able to tolerate life on the chalk, although they may not perform spectacularly.

There are, however, many alkaline soils which are deep and moisture retentive, not only in the British Isles but also in North America and Europe. On moisture-retentive soils with an alkalinity of up to pH 8 an extensive range of magnolias can be cultivated, although they would not succeed on thin dry soils of a similar pH value. No information is available on magnolia tolerance to higher levels of alkalinity. It seems apparent that moisture levels play a significant role in magnolia cultivation on alkaline sites. There is still the risk of chlorosis on alkaline soils, but the addition of a balanced fertilizer will rectify this problem.

Planting

Referring back to soil preparation, the planting pit will have been prepared, with copious quantities of well-rotted organic matter added. This site should be chosen with care, as it should also be the final position of the plant. I will not go into the detailed nitty gritty of planting and staking requirements as this is more than adequately covered in the majority of gardening books available today. Points to consider are as follows:

1 Incorporate up to 8oz per square yard (230gms per square metre) of a balanced inorganic fertilizer if planting in the spring.
2 Magnolias should never be planted too deep, the final level of soil being just proud of the top of the existing compost level.
3 Great care should be taken to avoid breaking any of the roots. Magnolias have a fleshy root system that, if not in active growth, will not heal over sufficiently quickly. A plant should be firmed in according to the prevailing soil conditions.
4 I prefer to plant out when the magnolia is small, between 18in (46cm) and 4ft (1.2m), depending on the variety. This way the magnolia will quickly adjust itself to the surrounding soil conditions.
5 Water the plant in well if planting during late spring or during the summer months.
6 March to the end of April is the optimum planting period, provided that a containerized plant has been given frost protection during the winter months. Late September to early November would be my second choice. Avoid the height of summer unless you can irrigate and January and February (in northern Europe and the British Isles) because of the likelihood of severe weather.

Transplanting

A fair amount of information has been written about the varying degrees of success achieved when transplanting magnolias from one site to another. Both J. G. Millais and Neil Treseder report considerable success in moving large specimens. The following are points for consideration if you are intending to move a large plant (the information refers to the moving of an 8ft (2.4m) by 8ft (2.4m) *M. stellata*).

1 Transplanting was carried out during open weather in March.
2 The crown was tied in and a trench opened up around the magnolia; this revealed a root ball 6ft (1.8m) across.
3 The root ball was gradually reduced in size with a fork, exposing the root network. Damaged roots were pruned, but the remainder were left. A 4½ft (1.4m) root ball remained. It was undercut and was not deeper than 15in (38cm). The root ball was wrapped in hessian to ensure that the root system neither dried out nor disintegrated.
4 The plant was moved into the prepared pit, the hessian was removed, and friable soil backfilled around the plant and firmed. The crown was then untied and reduced in size by about a quarter or a third. (Reducing the crown means that the plant will lose less water by transpiration and therefore recover more quickly.)
5 If a tree magnolia is moved, the tree should be guyed to ensure that the root system remains firmly anchored, essential for quick recovery.
6 If irrigation is on hand, this will certainly aid recovery if applied at regular intervals during the summer months.

Mulching

There is a wide range of suitable organic mulches (see page 99) that can be used effectively around magnolias. A 2in (5cm) layer of mulch spread over the top of the soil will hold additional moisture which may well prove crucial in times of drought. Provided it is weed free it also virtually eliminates the need to cultivate the soil around the base of the magnolia and cultivation is detrimental to both young and old plants because their fleshy roots resent disturbance.

Pruning

Generally speaking, magnolias do not need pruning as a regular cultivation requirement. It is only necessary if the plant has to be trained against a wall, becomes too large for its location in the garden, is mis-shapen, has been damaged, or has been transplanted.

E. A. Bowles in *My Garden in Spring* writes of pruning *M. stellata* at Myddleton House:

> I have only one specimen in the garden, but it is a large one, about 12 feet high by 13 feet through, being in the rock garden and so near a path I am obliged to cut off large boughs at times. It seems a dreadful thing to do, but if done early in the season, just after the last flowers have gone, the vigour of the new growths resulting from air and space and an extra allowance of sap, quite makes up for the removals, and the increase being in more convenient parts of the tree adds to the beauty and size of the specimen.

A good rule-of-thumb guide is to prune plants that flower in spring and early summer between mid-May and mid-July. Late-summer flowerers, such as *M. grandiflora*, should be pruned in the spring, when growth begins.

Magnolias often show considerable regenerative powers by throwing strong shoots from old wood. This can be advantageous in the event of branches being torn off by strong winds or for reshaping mis-shapen plants. If new shoots are selected to regrow in the affected areas, little damage will be evident several years later.

A wall subject, such as *M. grandiflora*, should be trained up for approximately two thirds of its ultimate height on a central leader, with only the main laterals being held in.

Fertilizers

Coming, as many of them do, from wooded or forested areas, magnolias are plants that perform well given high nutrient levels. To maintain their vigour and health we need to provide them with the right amounts of nitrogen, phosphorus, and potassium. Nitrogen promotes strong shoot growth and gives the plants a greater tolerance to drought and low temperatures. Phosphorus is beneficial for flower-bud production. Potassium ripens the current season's growth shoots and, with magnesium, is particularly useful in reducing chlorosis.

A range of proprietary quick- and slow-release inorganic fertilizers is available. Quick-release organic fertilizers are beneficial when applied in early spring, and dried blood is a useful additive.

Magnolia Species

Magnolia acuminata (the Cucumber Tree)

Magnolia acuminata is a large, elegant, fast-growing deciduous tree which is widely distributed in North America from Lake Erie in Canada through western New York, Oklahoma, and Arkansas to Louisiana and northern Florida. Its introduction to the British Isles is well documented. Peter Collinson, a Quaker linen draper from London was a garden enthusiast to whom like-minded people in America sent seeds and plants. One of these was John Bartram, a Quaker farmer, amateur physician, and self-taught botanist from Pennsylvania, who in July 1743 set out on a long journey from Pennsylvania to Lake Ontario. He kept a journal of this journey, three copies of which were sent to Collinson. Two never reached him, being taken by French privateers. The third, which was published by Collinson in 1751 under the title *Observations . . . made on his travels from Pensilvania to the Lake Ontario*, documents the discovery of *M. acuminata*. Its seeds were included in a selection of 100 species of seeds (mainly trees) that Bartram sent in a number of boxes to Collinson, who then distributed them to his patrons, who included the dukes of Richmond, Bedford, and Norfolk and Lord Bute, who supplied the Dowager Princess of Wales with plants for Kew. Each box was initially priced at 5 guineas, which soon increased to 10. *M. acuminata* duly flowered for Collinson at Mill Hill on 20 May 1762.

In cultivation it develops into a large tree of pyramidal outline which broadens with age. In the British Isles it grows to nearly 100ft (30m), but it reaches its greatest height in the southern Appalachian Mountains. The largest specimen on record is 125ft (38m) in height and has a spread of 60ft (18m); it was found in the Great Smoky Mountains National Park in Tennessee.

The green leaves are ovate, up to 10in (25m) long and about half as wide, and are slightly downy on the underside, especially along the midrib. The plant gets its specific name from the shape of the leaves, which taper to a point at the apex in the form termed 'acuminate'.

The erectly held, slightly fragrant flowers are rather small and insignificant, up to 3in (7.5cm) tall. They occur on leafy shoots from late May to July. In colour they are a mixture of glaucous green and yellow, but specific colour forms can be found varying from a blue through to a yellow. A distinctly yellow-flowered form, *M. acuminata* var. *aurea*, has been collected from the Carolinas, Tennessee, Georgia, and possibly Alabama.

This yellow coloration of the flower was thought to be a potential gene source to raise a yellow-flowered hybrid on leafless stems. In 1977, the Brooklyn Botanic Garden patented 'Elizabeth', a hybrid between *M. acuminata* and *M. denudata* (see page 70). Other interesting yellow-flowered hybrids have been produced, including 'Yellow Bird' (*M. acuminata* × *M.* × *brooklynensis*) and 'Yellow Lantern' (*M. acuminata* × *M.* × *soulangiana* 'Alexandrina'), a tree upright in habit with lemon-yellow flowers as large as 'Alexandrina'.

The popular name, Cucumber Tree, refers to the shape and colour of the fruits when they are young. These turn from bright green to red in autumn, but are not produced in sufficient quantity or size (3in, 7.5cm) to rank as an ornamental feature.

It is a fast-growing species, regularly increasing by between 18in (45cm) and 30in (75cm) a year. It is probably the hardiest magnolia species, being quoted as zone 4 in North America; the hardiest forms of all probably come from those plants found in New York State. In North America it is widely planted because of its ability to grow in a wide range of its soils, including alkaline ones, but it is not tolerant of drought. In its native environment it grows in deep, rich, moist soils with other deciduous trees such as *Acer saccharum* (the Sugar Maple) and *Quercus alba* (the White Oak). The timber is light and durable, close-grained, and of a light yellow-brown colour. It was formerly used by the North American Indians to make canoes and wooden bowls and is still not infrequently used for flooring and for joinery and other cabinet work.

Magnolia campbellii

This large deciduous tree (see pages 42, 44, 49) is native to the Himalayas from eastern Nepal, Sikkim, and Bhutan to Assam and is most common between 8,000ft (2,400m) and 10,000ft (3,000m). It is an aristocrat among the magnolia species. The English plant collector Frank Kingdon Ward, in *Plant Hunting on the Edge of the World*, paints a vivid picture of this plant and its habitat in Sikkim:

> The road cleaves to the face of the cliff, winding round and round, ever ascending towards the distant snows, while the valley fades beneath us. At last the air grows colder, for it is only March, and we reach the zone of oaks and rhododendrons. Everything is padded in moss; long wisps of it swing from the branches of the trees. A thin mist floats ghost-like through the dripping forest. Suddenly round a corner we come on that first Magnolia in full bloom. It is just below us and we look right into the heart of the tree, spouting with blossom. The sight overwhelms us. After that we see scores of trees, some with glowing pink, others with ivory-white flowers. From our giddy ledge we look down over the wide waves of the forest beating against the cliff, where the Magnolia blooms toss like white horses, or lie like a fleet of pink water lilies riding at anchor in a green surf.

In cultivation *Magnolia campbellii* is variable in habit, being a single-stemmed plant when young but quickly branching to become a tree of pyramidal outline. Some older trees can be of a sprawling habit, not tall but extremely wide – an advantage to the gardener, who is able to look down into the blooms. In cultivation, plants have reached a height of 70ft (21m) in southwest England; in the wild, plants of over 120ft (37m) have been reported from Bhutan. The growth rate in young trees is often quite vigorous – 3ft (90cm) to 4ft (120cm) per year is not uncommon.

The green leaves are up to 10in (25cm) long and 5in (12.5cm) wide, elliptic in shape. The undersides are coated with fine flattened hairs, especially along the midrib and main veins. The flower buds are also distinctive, being quite hairy and conical in shape. Flowers appear on leafless branches from February to the end of March, dependent on site and season. The 12 to 16 tepals are usually clear pink in colour, but they can vary from pure white, referred to a *M. campbellii* var. *alba* (see pages 42, 43), to crimson. They are slightly fragrant. In the wild the white and pink forms are mostly found in equal numbers, although in Nepal the white is dominant. Until the 1970s, the white form was not common in cultivation, but the introduction of white-flowered forms collected by Roy Lancaster, Tony Schilling, and Geoffrey Herklots from Nepal has gone some way to redress the balance. As the flowers expand they become bowl-shaped, with the outer tepals often reflexing like saucers to 10in (25cm) across. The inner tepals remain upright, enclosing the stamens and stigmatic column. Cut specimens brought into the house often open out fully like giant water lilies, presumably because of the significant rise in temperature.

Variability of flower colour has led to a number of named clones, available from specialist nurseries. 'Darjeeling' is an exceptionally dark pink or wine coloured form, vegetatively propagated from a tree growing in the Lloyd Botanic Garden, Darjeeling, India. 'Betty Jessel' is from the same tree in Darjeeling but was seed raised. According to Neil Treseder it is the nearest colour to crimson yet seen in a magnolia. It is a particularly late-flowering form.

A range of spectacular *M. campbellii* hybrids (other than those with *M. campbellii* var. *mollicomata*) can be found, with 'Princess Margaret' (see page 46) and 'Michael Rosse' (both *M.c.* var. *alba* × *M. sargentiana* var. *robusta*) and 'Star Wars' (*M. campbellii* × *M. liliiflora*) being of particular note.

M. × *veitchii* (*M. campbellii* × *M. denudata*), as well as being an impressive plant in its own right, is an important stepping stone in the breeding programme of the Gresham hybrids (see pages 121–3).

Seed-raised *M. campbellii* takes up to 30 years before flowering begins. For this reason selected clones are grafted or chip budded on to *M.c.* var. *mollicomata* as a root stock. These will generally flower in less than half the time.

Being one of the earliest magnolias to flower, *M. campbellii* is susceptible to frosting of the blooms, which bleaches out the colour, so it is important to site it where it will suffer least from frost. A sheltered yet sunny site with adequate frost drainage is especially useful here.

If a walled site is to be considered, the north wall should be chosen. The heat from the west wall will cause the buds to burst too early, making them more likely to become frosted. In North America, *M. campbellii* and its allies equate roughly with hardiness zone 7.

It is surprisingly wind tolerant, with many trees suffering only from minor branch breaks in the hurricane force winds that swept southeast England in October 1987.

Magnolia campbellii *var.* mollicomata

This large deciduous tree, the eastern form of *Magnolia campbellii*, comes from southeast Tibet, northern Burma, and western Yunnan. George Forrest, the Scottish plant collector, found it growing at an altitude of 10,000ft (3,000m). Frank Kingdon Ward also found it growing gregariously in the Seinghku Valley in upper Burma, where he saw trees over 100ft (30m) in height.

In cultivation, *M. campbellii* var. *mollicomata* grows in much the same way as its western brother, but its crown has a tendency to spread from an early age. The leaves are similar in outline to those of *M. campbellii* and have the same flattened hairs on the undersides. One of the main botanical distinctions between the two forms is the shape and size of the flower buds; those of var. *mollicomata* are larger, oblong in shape, and have hairy internodes on flowering stems; those of *M. campbellii* are glabrous.

Horticulturally, *M.c.* var. *mollicomata* takes less than half the time of *M. campbellii* to flower, with 10 to 14 years being quoted. Flower shape is sufficiently distinctive, with *M.c.* var. *mollicomata* always being a beautiful cup-and-saucer shape, the outer tepals remaining horizontal and the inner tepals forming a bulbous dome. The sizes when the flowers are open are comparable. The flowers of *M.c.* var. *mollicomata* are rose or rose-purple in colour (never a clear pink as in *M. campbellii*). Flowering time is April into early May, significantly later than *M. campbelli*, and consequently missing many early frosts. Fruiting is not normally an attraction with *M. campbellii* but it is with *M.c.* var. *mollicomata*, which bears long, bright red fruits in early autumn.

Particular mention should be made of *M.c.* var. *mollicomata* 'Lanarth' (see page 50) which is distinctive enough to warrant separate botanical ranking within the *M. campbellii* complex. It was collected by George Forrest in 1924 from northwest Yunnan on the Salween-Kiu Chiang Divide in open thickets at an altitude of between 10,000ft (3,000m) and 11,000ft (3,350m). Only three seedlings were raised, and named after the English gardens where they were planted – Lanarth and Werrington in Cornwall and Borde Hill in Sussex. Both Cornish gardens were owned at the time by the Williams family, who affectionately knew the plant as 'The Magnolia with a telephone number' – a reference to the George Forrest collection number, 25655. 'Lanarth' can be distinguished from other members of the species in a number of different ways, of which the most recognizable are:

a) The parent plant exhibits vigorous fastigiate growth.

b) The leaves are similar in length but very much broader, oblong obovate in shape, and thicker in texture.

c) The flower buds are much larger and flatter.

d) The cup-and-saucer shape of the flower is typical of *M.c.* var. *mollicomata*, but the colour, an incredible lilac-purple-red, is most distinctive.

e) Flowering occurs at the same time as *M. campbellii*.

f) Budded propagules show a markedly different growth response as compared with *M. campbellii* and *M.c.* var. *mollicomata*, showing a reluctance to grow. Seedlings, however, exhibit a vigour similar to that of the parent tree.

Magnolia campbellii × Magnolia campbellii *var.* mollicomata

Charles Raffill of the Royal Botanic Gardens, Kew, in 1946, and Sir Charles Cave of Sidbury Manor, Devon, prior to 1946, working independently, both crossed the two races of *Magnolia campbellii*. The resulting cross produced flowers that combined the bright pink colour of *M. campbellii* with the graceful cup-and-saucer shape of *M. campbellii* var. *mollicomata*.

The first seedling to gain recognition was one sent to the gardens of Windsor Great Park, where it flowered after 13 years from the seedling stage. It was subsequently named 'Charles Raffill' after the originator of the cross and went on to receive a Preliminary Commendation in 1961, an Award of Merit in 1963, and a First Class Certificate in 1966.

Other seedlings in this group include 'Kew's Surprise' (see page 48), which exhibits most sensationally the cup-and-saucer effect.

Magnolia enthusiasts in North America have continued this hybridization programme. *M. campbellii* 'Eric Walther' is reported to be of this parentage, with rose-pink flowers. This is named after the first Director of the Strybing Arboretum, San Francisco, where it is planted.

Magnolia cordata

Magnolia cordata (see page 58) is very variable in habit, from a slow-growing large, spreading shrub to a medium-sized tree of upright growth. An American species, it has a restrictive distribution, being found in the southern states of Georgia, Alabama, the Carolinas, and Florida. It was discovered near Augusta, Georgia, by André Michaux (or perhaps his son Francois) between the years 1787 and 1796 and was sent to France in 1803. But two Scots, John Fraser and John Lyon, who were collecting at the same time and more or less in the same area as Michaux, are reported to have introduced the species into the British Isles some two years earlier, in 1801. *M. cordata* was known only by these introductions until 1910, when Louis A. Berckmans stumbled on a group of shrubs varying between 4ft (1.2m) and 6ft (1.8m) in height in dry oak woodland some 18 miles south of Atlanta.

The botanical world is still debating whether *M. cordata* should be reclassified as simply a subspecies of *M. acuminata*. Many plants in cultivation are slow-growing, large-spreading shrubs, but a number of trees between 40ft (12m) and 50ft (15m) in height can be found.

The leaves are 6in (15m) long and up to 4in (10cm) wide and generally elliptic in shape (rarely cordate as the name implies). The shoots are also pubescent for a short distance behind the main growth bud. Tulip-shaped flowers, up to 4in (12cm) across, are borne on leafy shoots during late May and June and sometimes into early July, but are never profusely produced in the British Isles. The colour varies from a pale to a canary yellow, often with reddish lines on the inner tepals. 'Miss Honeybee' is an exceptionally fine yellow-flowered form which blooms from an early age. The fruits are reported to be smaller and a brighter red than those of *M. acuminata*.

A shrub with tremendous potential for the future has been raised by P. Savage of Michigan. As yet unnamed, the shrub bears yellow blooms on bare stems; each flower has been likened to a gardenia in both shape and poise. The parentage is *M. acuminata* 'Miss Honeybee' and *M. stellata* 'Rubra'.

M. cordata is, like *M. acuminata*, tolerant of alkaline soils. The soil must, however, be moisture retentive, when good growth can be expected (up to 15in (38cm) per year). A warm sunny site is also required. In America it is hardiness rated as zone 7.

Magnolia cylindrica

Magnolia cylindrica (see page 64) is a slow-growing small tree, generally of a spreading habit, which comes from Anhwei Province in eastern China. It was discovered by R. C. Ching on the Wang Shan at an elevation of 4,200ft (1,280m) in 1925 and was named by E. H. Wilson in 1927. It did not reach Western gardens until 1936, when the late Mrs J. Norman Henry of Gladwyne, Pennsylvania, received seed from the Lu Shan Botanic Garden in China. Seeds were sent to gardens in the British Isles at the same time, but they failed to germinate. Mrs Henry's seed germinated, was grown on, and distributed as scions to the University of Washington Arboretum in Seattle and also to the late Sir Harold Hillier in about 1950. Hillier also received scions in 1951/52 from F. M. Kluis Nursery of Pompton Lakes, New Jersey (late of Boskoop).

There are two distinct forms in cultivation. The one more generally seen is a slow-growing tree of a spreading and arching habit often as broad as it is tall. A specimen in the Hillier Gardens and Arboretum is 16ft (5m) tall by as much across after some twenty years. The other form is taller and more upright. It may well be that the two forms originate in the two sources of the scions received by Hilliers in the early 1950s.

The leaves vary in size to a maximum of 6in (15cm) by 3in (7.5cm). They are dark green above and smell of aniseed when crushed. The 4in (10cm) candle-like flowers are pure white with delicate rays of pale pink at the base; they open during April. Flowers show a remarkable tolerance to frost. A specimen at Chyverton in Devon is reported to have suffered no damage when exposed to ground frost at 10.4°F (−12°C), although it had already broken bud. The plants themselves also come through severe weather virtually unscathed. There are instances of the species surviving −22°F (−30°C) in eastern North America (zone 4).

During late September and early October the 4in (10cm) long, bright red cylindrical fruiting cones that give the plant its specific name are an attractive feature.

M. cylindrica grows well in a rich, moist, acid soil in light dappled shade. However, I see no reason why this species cannot grow (like its Chinese cousins, although perhaps not so well) on an alkaline soil, provided that it is moisture retentive.

'Albatross' (*M. cylindrica* × *M.* × *veitchii*) is a fast-growing tree of upright habit which is a spectacular sight in April, when large, pure white flowers can be seen in profusion.

Magnolia dawsoniana

During his third expedition to China in 1908, E. H. Wilson discovered this species (see page 52) in western Szechwan Province near Tatsien-lu. He sent the fruit to the Arnold Arboretum in Massachusetts. Seedlings were raised along with Wilson's other Chinese species but the young plants succumbed to Boston's harsh winter. In 1913 Professor Charles Sargent, the Arnold Arboretum's director, took the bold step of sending this species along with Wilson's other magnolia introductions to Léon Chenault, who ran a famous nursery at Orleans, France. Chenault successfully grafted Wilson's collection and distributed plants to Kew and later to a number of other gardens in the British Isles. One of these was Rowallane in Northern Ireland, where *Magnolia dawsoniana* flowered in about 1932.

M. dawsoniana grows into a small-to-medium tree of a broad pyramidal outline, with a 'twiggy' network of branches. Rates of growth vary, averaging from 12in (30cm) to 24in (60cm) per year. The dark green leaves are roughly oval in outline, up to 6in (15cm) long by 2in (5cm) to 3in (7.5cm) wide, and have distinctive net-veining on the upper and lower surfaces.

Pale pink, faintly fragrant flowers are produced on leafless stems towards the end of March, in April, and often into early May. The nine horizontally held tepals are more attractive when in bud as they hang limply when they are fully open.

A more spectacular colour form is 'Chyverton', named after the famous Cornish garden where it flowered for the first time in 1967, some twenty-three years after raising. On first opening, the flowers are bright crimson; the colour seems to become more pronounced during cold weather. The blooms are remarkably frost tolerant and last for about six weeks. Some authorities consider 'Chyverton' to be a hybrid with *M. sprengeri* 'Diva'.

Today most plants of *M. dawsoniana* are either grafted or budded, thus considerably reducing the time taken for flowering to start, with ten years from propagation being about average.

Like most magnolias, the species needs a moisture-retentive soil to flourish. It prefers a soil on the acid side of neutral, but is surprisingly tolerant of alkaline sites. Plenty of space in full sun is also needed for this plant to develop to its potential. In America it is quoted as hardiness zone 7, although 'Chyverton' is thought to be hardier than the species.

Magnolia delavayi

This imposing evergreen tree (see page 61) was discovered in the Chinese Himalaya by the French missionary and plant collector Père Jean Delavay in 1886. It was a further 13 years before it was introduced into cultivation by Ernest Wilson, who collected seed during the autumn of 1899 from southern Yunnan, where it was growing in sandstone and limestone formations among Lithocarpus scrub.

In cultivation it grows into a broad, spreading, multi-stemmed large shrub or, in the south and southeast of England, into a small to medium tree. It rarely has a stem, branching more or less from ground level.

The elegant, matt green leaves are up to 15in (36cm) long and 8in (20cm) wide and are some of the largest leaves seen among temperate evergreen trees. The leaves are held fairly rigidly on the tree, so it is difficult for the viewer to appreciate fully the glaucous underside, which contrasts well with the upper surface.

The flowers are a disappointment – they last only for a few hours and are fully open only at night. They are ivory-white in colour, fragrant (most noticeably so at night), and when fully open are 7in (18cm) across. The flowers appear sporadically from July onwards and can be seen into September. Raised from seed, *Magnolia delavayi* flowers after 10 years when about 12ft (3.7m) in height. It does not normally fruit in the British Isles but in California large red fruiting cones are sparsely produced.

M. delavayi is surprisingly frost tolerant considering that it comes from altitudes below 10,000ft (3,000m) in China; it shows no adverse effects to 7°C (–14°C) in the British Isles (hardiness zone 7/8 in the USA). It may be grown in a variety of situations – used as a wall shrub or as a free-standing tree in an open woodland setting, where it is seen to advantage. During prolonged periods of severe winter weather, tip dieback or even defoliation can occur, but in the majority of instances regeneration occurs.

A remarkable wide range of soils will suit, from a thin chalk to a rich, acid, moisture-retentive loam (where it is most at home).

Magnolia denudata

Magnolia denudata, the Yulan or Lily Tree, is native to the central Chinese provinces of Anhwei, Chekiang, Kiangsi, and Hunan, where it is found growing in moist woodland. Buddhist monks have been cultivating this species for centuries and planted it extensively in their temple gardens. The earliest records indicating the significance of this plant to the Buddhists go back to the Tang Dynasty (AD 618–906), when the flower was regarded as a symbol of openness and purity. At this time, the Buddhist monks were taking their religious opinions to Japan, and they very probably took the Yulan also.

Sir Joseph Banks introduced the species to the British Isles in 1789, almost certainly from a cultivated source, but it remained uncommon in cultivation for many years. One famous early specimen was grown by Sir Abraham Hume at Wormleybury in Hertfordshire; in 1826 it measured 20ft (6m) in height and carried more than nine hundred blooms.

In cultivation *M. denudata* is often seen as a multi-stemmed shrub or broad, spreading, small tree; it often takes more than a hundred years to grow to 30ft (9m) in height and as much across. The green obovate leaves are up to 6in (15cm) long and 3in (7.5m) wide and have a fine coating of hairs on the underside. The species flowers young – plants only three or four years old flowering prolifically. It is also early flowering – from February to April dependent on the climate and the geographic location. The lemon-scented blooms consist of nine tepals forming erect chalices, 3in (7.5cm) to 4in (10cm) long, of pure white flowers which light up the garden at sunrise and sunset. The first flush of flower is particularly effective during a frost-free period, because the blooms are spoiled by frost, which results in browning of the tepal margins. This particular trait apart, the plant can tolerate exceptionally harsh conditions; in America it is quoted as hardiness zone 5. The brown fruiting cones, 5in (12.5cm) long, open to reveal bright red seeds.

M. denudata prefers a rich, moisture-retentive soil on the acid side of neutral. However, like a number of other Chinese species, it will tolerate alkaline conditions provided the soil does not dry out during the summer months. It should be given a sunny site or one in a light dappled shade.

The tepals of *M. denudata* are considered to be a delicacy. Dipped in flour and fried in oil until they are crisp, they have a slightly sweet taste.

Debate has raged in the botanical world over the naming of this species; many authorities have considered that it should correctly be called *M. heptapeta*. However, in a recent article, Frederick Meyer of the United States National Arboretum and Elizabeth McClintock of the University of California, have proved *M. denudata* of Desrousseaux (1791) to be the earliest applicable name for the species.

M. denudata is one of the parents of the all-important *M.* × *soulangiana* (see page 124) and, more recently, of 'Elizabeth' (see page 70). 'Purple Eye' (see page 65) is a beautiful clone with purple flushing at the base of the inner tepals, said to have arisen at Caerhays in Cornwall. It is a more vigorous plant than *M. denudata*, with larger leaves and flowers which open later and more widely. Some authorities consider it to be not a clone but a hybrid between *M. denudata* and *M.* × *soulangiana*.

Magnolia fraseri

This small-to-medium tree is native to the rich woods of the southern Appalachian region of eastern North America and is found in the states of Georgia, Alabama, Louisiana, West Virginia, Texas, South Carolina, and northwest Florida.

It is named after John Fraser, a Scot who went to London in 1770. Fraser made a number of collecting trips to North America in the 1780s and brought back the species to England in either 1784 or 1786. However it was William Bartram, son of John, who had first discovered the species, in South Carolina in 1776.

Magnolia fraseri is a fast-growing small-to-medium tree that reaches a height of 60ft (18m), but has been known to be taller. It often has multiple stems. It is found in the stream valleys and creeks to an altitude of 4,400ft (1,350m) and is often seen among the taller red maples and white oaks. The narrowly obovate-oblong, seagreen leaves up to 12in (30cm) long and 5in (12.5cm) wide are most distinctive, with auriculate lobes at the base which give rise to the tree's common name of Fishtail Magnolia. The leaves are characteristically crowded towards the end of the branches, giving a 'whorled' appearance. In autumn they turn a distinctive reddish-brown colour.

It is the first American species to flower, on leafy shoots during late May and June. The milky white flowers have eight tepals up to 4in (10cm) long which splay out to about 8in (20cm) across. As they open, the flowers have what has been described as a mild detergent scent.

The fruiting cones are decorative, being rosy red in colour and 5in (12.5cm) long. As seed germinates readily, this species is often used as an understock for grafting or budding. Even during the winter months the one-year-old shoots are quite decorative, their brown colour contrasting with the dark purple of the winter bud. Between 12in (30cm) and 24in (60cm) of growth is put on annually, so that in a score of years trees may be expected to grow to approximately 30ft (9m).

M. fraseri is perfectly hardy, growing well in full sun in the British Isles, although it will tolerate shady conditions, especially in its native country. A rich, moisture-retentive, acidic soil suits it, although it is known to grow in deep, moisture-retentive, alkaline soils in North America. It is quite hardy; in North America it is regarded as tolerating hardiness zone 5.

M. fraseri var. *pyramidata* is one of America's rarest magnolias and is seldom met with in cultivation outside its native environment. Compared with *M. fraseri* it is pyramidal in outline, more compact in habit, smaller in its floral parts, and less hardy. It comes from Florida and Texas; unsurprisingly, Texan trees are reported to carry larger flowers than those from Florida.

Magnolia globosa

This species is found as a large shrub or small tree, at altitudes between 8,000ft (2,400m) and 11,000ft (3,400m), over a wide geographic range, from eastern Nepal in the west to northwest Yunnan, China, in the east. There are distinctive botanical differences between the eastern and western forms, which in cultivation are known as the Indian form and the Chinese form.

The Chinese form was introduced into cultivation in July 1919 by George Forrest, who found it in the Tsarong region of southeast Tibet. Plants seen by Forrest were shrubs or small trees up to 20ft (6m) in height, with young shoots densely clothed with rust-coloured down. It was originally described as *Magnolia sarongensis*. The Indian form was introduced from Sikkim by Dr J. Cromar Watt of Aberdeen in 1930; it flowered in 1937. Dr Watt first saw it at Tonglu at 10,000ft (3,000m), 'the magnificent white oval buds standing erect on leafless branches, and the stem silhouetted against a background of Kinchinjunga's snows'. It is tree-like in habit, growing to 25ft (7.5m), with young shoots green and glabrous.

The foliage is oval, up to 10in (25cm) long by half as wide, silvery-grey between the veins on the Chinese form and golden on the Indian. The Chinese form starts into growth considerably earlier than the Indian.

In cultivation, the creamy white flowers, some 3in (7.5cm) across, are produced on leafy shoots in June. They are held either nodding or almost horizontal, which partially exposes a rich rose-red ring of stamens. They do not fully open, forming egg-shaped cups of nine tepals held in three whorls (which accounts for the Nepalese name, 'the Hen Magnolia'). The flowers are fragrant, most noticeably in the evening. The fruiting cones are reddish-brown, pendulous, and up to 2½in (6cm) in length.

The Indian form is considerably hardier than the Chinese, the latter being suitable only for the mildest of localities. Both forms are best grown in a sheltered, shaded environment in a rich, leafy, moisture-retentive soil. The Indian form could be considered as hardiness zone 7.

Magnolia grandiflora
This 'elegant aristocrat of American trees' is a large, handsome, evergreen tree from the southeastern United States, from North Carolina south to central Florida and west to eastern Texas and Arkansas. It grows only within a few hundred miles of the Atlantic Ocean or the Gulf of Mexico. It can be found along the bluffs of the lower Mississippi river and on the borders of river swamps and ponds in association with the water oak (*Quercus nigra*), *Liquidambar styraciflua*, and *Nyssa sylvatica*. It was commonly planted in front of early homesteads in the south, often with the lower branches pegged down so that they rooted as layers. This practice not only provided replacement plants, but also made the tree virtually impregnable against the prevalent hurricane-force winds even at their most vicious.

In their native environment trees reach 90ft (37.5m) in height. In the southeast of England 40ft (12m) is the most that can be expected, but sites in the south of France or Italy bordering on the Riviera produce specimens as large as those found in North America. In cultivation, *Magnolia grandiflora* is variable in leaf, flower, shape, size, and habit, and 150 named varieties are quoted. Leaves are generally oval in shape, up to 10in (25m) long and less than half as wide, and tapered at both ends. They are leathery in texture, dark glossy green above, and often have a thick, red-brown, felt-like indumentum beneath.

The large creamy white flowers have a lemon fragrance and are of a size in keeping with the majestic foliage – often up to 14in (36cm) across. They vary in the number of tepals (nine and more) and last only for two days, being cup-shaped on the first and saucer-shaped on the second. In America the flowers are generally seen during May and June.

Seedling-raised trees begin to flower from twenty years old; vegetatively propagated plants flower earlier, from five years. *M. grandiflora* seldom bears fruiting cones in the British Isles, needing the heat of its native country in order to produce them.

It is one of the most temperature tolerant of temperate broadleaved evergreen plants. It can grow happily in tropical climates but is able to withstand temperatures down to −11°F (−24°C), dependent on the variety, for short periods of time (hardiness zone 6). In the British Isles prolonged periods at 74°F (−14°C) will defoliate young plants (other than those noted for their tolerance of low temperatures), but mature plants will be unscathed. In its native environment it lives with temperatures down to 10°F (−12°C). It tolerates a wide range of soil types – almost anything except a thin, dry, alkaline soil will sustain it. It will grow happily in sun or semi-shade.

There are a large number of cultivars. The following represent some of the more popular named forms.

'Angustifolia' is distinct on account of its narrow lanceolate leaves, to 8in (20cm) long by 4½in (11cm) wide, which are glossy green above with a light cinnamon colouring beneath which disappears with age. It is said to have originated in France in 1825.

'Exmouth' is the oldest of the English cultivars. It was introduced in the early part of the 18th century and takes its name from the Devonshire town where Sir John Colliton grew it. It is vigorous and erect in growth with elliptic leaves waxy green above with a reddish-brown indumentum beneath, which is lost with age. The flowers are very large, with 18 tepals, and appear from an early age.

'Ferruginea' is an erect form of compact habit which has a rich rust-coloured indumentum on the underside of the leaf. The flowers are typical in size and are produced freely when the plant is growing in a sunny site. It is often recommended for chalky soils.

'Goliath', an extremely popular cultivar in the British Isles, is of bushy habit with oval leaves up to 8in (20cm) in length, with virtually no indumentum on the underside of the leaf. It produces (although not prolifically) globular flowers, up to 12in (30cm) across when fully open, over a long period from August to November (in the British Isles).

'Little Gem' is a slow-growing compact tree of distinctive columnar habit, which according to reports is only 14ft (4.25m) in height and 4ft (1.2m) across after 16 years. The leaves are elliptic in shape, 5in (12.5cm) by 2in (5cm), dark green above with a good rust-coloured indumentum beneath. The flowers are cup-shaped with a tendency to remain this shape as opposed to opening saucer-like on the second day. It is an American introduction named in 1906.

'St. Mary' grows quite distinctively into a large bushy shrub with waxy, rich green leaves which have a particularly dark indumentum on their undersides. The foliage is also wavy margined. The flowers are freely produced from an early age. This is an American cultivar named by W. B. Clarke and Co. of San Jose, California, after the Glen St Mary Nursery, Florida, from which it was purchased.

'Samuel Sommer' is one of the finest selections, being of sturdy erect growth with large, very glossy, green leaves above and an excellent golden-rusty-brown indumentum on the underside. The flowers are exceptionally large, even from an early age – 12in (30cm) across initially, they can reach 15in (39cm) across in favoured locations on well-established plants. Neil Treseder reports this form to have survived tornado winds and temperatures of −12°F (−24.4°C) at Reinhardt College in Georgia. It was raised by the Saratoga Horticultural Foundation and named after the President of the Board of Trustees in 1952.

Magnolia hypoleuca

This large, fast-growing deciduous tree is found in the forested mountainous regions of the Russian Kuril Islands and southward through the Japanese Islands of Hokkaido to the Ryuku Islands. Along with *Magnolia kobus*, its natural distribution is probably the most northerly of all magnolia species.

In cultivation it develops into an upright tree of only medium size, though it grows considerably larger in the Forests of Hokkaido, Japan, where specimens of over 100ft (30m) have been found.

The leaves are obovate in shape and can reach 18in (46m) in length by 8in (20cm) in width when planted in a favourable site. As the young leaves unfold, a fine pubescence creates a silvery green colour on the underside of the leaf, which with age changes to a grey-green. The creamy white flowers appear on leafy shoots during June and early July and are richly scented. The nine tepals are generally cup-shaped when they open, but become saucer-shaped, up to 8in (20cm) across. Some of the outer tepals are often tinged with pink as the flower ages. A few trees have been noted to have flowers which are distinctly pink. This species flowers from a comparatively early age, at 12 to 15 years. The heavily scented blooms of midsummer are followed by richly coloured scarlet fruits, approximately 7in (18cm) long, during September and early October. By mid-November these become a light brown in colour.

In the south and southwest of England, *M. hypoleuca* is a fast-growing tree. It puts on between 2ft (60cm) and 4ft (90cm) of growth per year when young, especially if growing in a sunny yet sheltered site in a rich, moisture-retentive, slightly acid soil. It is surprisingly hardy, being regarded as zone 5 in North America.

The timber is soft, close-grained, and a pale yellowish-brown in colour. It is used extensively in Japan for furniture and cabinet work.

M. hypoleuca has been crossed with another Japanese species, *M. sieboldii*, to produce an extravagantly scented shrub called *M.* × *wieseneri* (see pages 127–8) and with *M. tripetala* to produce 'Silver Parasol'.

Magnolia kobus

In cultivation *Magnolia kobus* (see page 78) is most frequently seen as a small-to-medium tree, initially pyramidal in outline, which becomes with age a broad, spreading tree. It is common throughout the forests of Japan as well as on the isolated volcanic island of Cheju-do (Quelpart Island), off the south coast of Korea.

It was first introduced into North America during the winter of 1861 by Dr. George Hall of Rhode Island, who passed it on to the Parsons Brothers, nurserymen of Flushing, Long Island, as *M. thurberi*. It was almost certainly collected from plants growing on the island of Honshu. Seeds from plants growing in Sapporo on the island of Hokkaido were later sent to the Arnold Arboretum in 1876 by William Clark, the first president of the Massachusetts Agricultural College. However it was not until about 1879 that it was introduced into the British Isles, when Charles Maries, an English plant collector, brought back seed to be grown at Veitch's Coombe Wood Nursery.

With such a widespread distribution it can vary considerably in habit, from a large multi-stemmed shrub to a fine tree some 75ft (23in) in height. Many authorities regard the robust tree form found in forests on the Island of Hokkaido as *M. kobus* var. *borealis*, but George Johnstone in 1950 and Stephen Spongberg in 1976 both rejected this view on the grounds that there are no clearcut characteristics distinguishing the forms. Growth rates vary considerably, with as much as 2½ft (25cm) being seen on young and vigorous trees.

The winter buds are quite distinctive, being very downy. The leaves are up to 6in (15cm) long by 3in (7.5cm) at their widest point and are obovate in shape. Both the leaves and the young stems emit a distinctive smell of aniseed when crushed, but this is not nearly so distinctive as with *M. salicifolia*.

The white flowers (often with a hint of pink at the base of the tepals) appear on leafless shoots from early March to early April, dependent on site and season. The six tepals are generally quite small, up to 4in (10cm), and the flowers retain a vase shape up to maturity. Occasional trees produce flowers that open completely, but these are probably *M. kobus* hybrids (*M.* × *loebneri* and 'Kewensis'). The flowers are frost sensitive – because the first flush of flower also happens to be the main flush, a frost of only a few degrees (to 10°F, −7°C) can have a disastrous effect, with the tepals becoming completely browned. The fruiting cones are not particularly attractive – they are green initially, eventually turning russet brown, and about 5in (18cm) long. *M. kobus* produces seed quite freely, especially when grown in association with other plants of the same or a closely related species. Plants raised from seed are often used for understocks in the nursery trade.

This is a particularly useful plant because it adapts uncomplainingly to a wide range of soil types, including the alkaline. It does not do well, however, in thin, dry soils, presumably because its home is in moisture-retentive, humus-rich sites in Japan. Apart from the flowers, the plant is particularly hardy, surviving temperatures reportedly as low as −29°F (−34°C) (US hardiness zone 4).

The wood is soft, close-grained, and a light yellow in colour. In Japan it has been used for making matches as well as kitchen utensils. The bark is used in medicinal preparations by the Ainu as a cold cure.

M. kobus has been crossed with *M. stellata* and *M. salicifolia* to produce *M.* × *loebneri* and 'Kewensis' respectively (see page 123).

It is very variable in its time taken to flower, with 7 to 30 years from seed being quoted; vegetatively propagated material, however, flowers within 10 years of propagation.

Some botanical authorities now suggest that the correct name for *M. kobus* is *M. praecosissima*.

Magnolia liliiflora

The Mu-lan or Woody Orchid (so called because of its orchid-like flowers borne on woody stems) is a medium-to-large shrub of an open, sprawling habit. This species has been cultivated in both China and Japan for centuries but it is considered to be native only to the warm temperate regions of eastern and central China. Ernest Wilson and George Forrest sent back herbarium specimens of the species in 1900 and 1910 respectively, but the third Duke of Portland had already introduced it many years before, in 1790, from a cultivated plant growing in Japan.

It is a slow-growing, multi-stemmed shrub. Once established it will grow up to 1ft (30cm) per year in favourable locations. Specimens of up to 12ft (3.5cm) in height and as much across can be seen; these are upwards of 20 years of age.

The dark green leaves are generally oblong or ovate in shape and 7in (18cm) long by 4in (10cm) wide. When young they are downy on the underside but by the middle of the season the downiness is visible only along the midrib.

The flowers, 4in (10cm) high, are a vinous purple and white on the outside and white inside. They bloom from late April and peak in mid-to-late May, although they can continue into June. They are normally chalice-shaped but are often looser, when they look rather like an untidy tulip.

There are a number of different forms. Probably the best known in the British Isles is 'Nigra', a more robust and more upright form than the type, with larger flowers, darker purple externally and a curious white-purple inside. This form is regarded by many as having the longest flowering period of all magnolias, with flowers occurring sporadically often into the autumn. Of the North American selections, 'O'Neill' was selected by the late Professor Joe McDaniel of the University of Illinois for its vigorous habit and large, dark purple flowers. This may be outstanding in North America, but it has not proved to be an improvement over 'Nigra' in the British Isles.

M. liliiflora and its forms are excellent subjects for the smaller garden, either as lawn specimens or as border plants. They generally like a sheltered yet sunny position in a moisture-retentive soil on the acid side of neutral. 'Nigra' and 'O'Neill' are regarded as hardier forms, being graded as US hardiness zone 6, while *M. liliiflora* itself is considered to be zone 7. In the British Isles 'Nigra' is regarded as the most satisfactory choice for cultivating because of its extra vigour and extended flowering period.

This is an extremely important parent species in magnolia breeding programmes. It has been used extensively, most famously in work on *M.* × *soulangiana* (see page 124), but more recently it has been widely used in North America to produce the small de Vos and Kosar hybrids (see page 120) and the Gresham hybrids (see page 121).

It has been known by a number of synonymous names, including *M. purpurea*, *M. discolor*, and, most recently, *M. quinquepeta*, but in a recent publication Frederick G. Meyer and Elizabeth McClintock have come down in favour of *M. liliiflora* of Desrousseaux (1791) as the earliest applicable name.

Magnolia macrophylla

The Big Leaf Magnolia is generally a small-to-medium, broad-spreading, multi-stemmed tree. It has a restricted distribution in the southeastern United States, being found in Georgia, Alabama, and Louisiana and northwards to west Virginia, Kentucky, and Arkansas.

It was first discovered by André Michaux in the mountains of South Carolina in 1759 and seems to have been introduced into the British Isles in 1800.

In its native habitat it is a small-to-medium tree, varying in size from 25ft (7.5m) to 50ft (15m) and in habit from a single erect to a multi-stemmed spreading crown. In the British Isles it seldom reaches a height of more than 40ft (12m).

This is a most remarkable species on account of its sensational foliage – the largest of all the magnolia species – which in its native habitat can attain up to 3ft (90cm) in length and 1ft (30cm) in width. Climatic conditions in the British Isles do not allow such sizes to be reached, but the leaves can still be 24in (60cm) long. Despite their size, the leaves have a rather flimsy, papery appearance; they are green above and a silvery chalky white beneath. They are oblong obovate in shape and tend to be concentrated towards the ends of the branches.

The fragrant flowers are of a similar size to those of *Magnolia grandiflora*, being cup-shaped and up to 12in (30cm) across. They are composed of six fleshy tepals, creamy white in colour and often with some purple spotting towards the centre of the flower. They are seen during May in North America and have been said to 'shine out through the forest in spite of the huge leafy parasols on which they nestle'. *M. macrophylla* does not flower prolifically in the

British Isles, because of the comparatively cool summer temperatures. The fruits are cone-like, up to 3in (7.5cm) long, and reddish-pink fading to a pale brown in colour.

This rare tree is found either individually or in small groups in sheltered woodlands, especially in ravines and river valleys along with *Liquidambar* (Sweet Gum), *Liriodendron* (Tulip Tree), and *Quercus texana* (Southern Red Oak). Rich, deep, moisture-retentive soils either just on the acid or just on the alkaline side of neutral are best for this species, which requires also a sunny yet sheltered site, otherwise the flamboyant foliage display will be severely reduced.

Provided effective ripening of the wood takes place, *M. macrophylla* is quite hardy, being regarded in the United States as hardiness zone 5. Far too often growth in the British Isles continues well into the autumn, causing frosting of the new growth to hamper the tree's development. It also needs hot summers to make good growth.

M. macrophylla subsp. *ashei* is regarded as America's rarest magnolia. It is found in the lowlands of northwest Florida, where it attains a height of 20ft (6m). *Ostrya virginiana* (the American Hop Hornbeam) and *Aesculus pavia* (the Red Buckeye) are found growing in association with it. It differs from the type by having narrower fruit and smaller flowers, which even in the British Isles are seen on plants of five or so years of age. A plant in the Hillier Gardens and Arboretum is some 8ft (2.5m) in height and flowers regularly, up to 10 in (25cm) across, during July. It is regarded as tender, but it has not suffered when exposed to temperatures down to 7°F (−14°C) (US hardiness zone 7). George Johnstone introduced it into the British Isles in 1949 and flowered it some four years later.

Magnolia nitida

This erect-growing evergreen shrub (in cultivation) or ultimately a large tree (in the wild) is native to northwest Yunnan, China, Upper Burma, and southeast Tibet.

It was discovered by George Forrest in 1917 on the Mekong-Salween Divide in northwest Yunnan at an altitude of between 10,000ft (3,000m) and 11,000ft (3,350m). Reginald Farrer found the species in 1919 in Upper Burma around Hpimaw, in 'a frontier outpost bordering north west Yunnan where it was growing at 8,000 feet on the fringes of the forest with a bitter winter and a complete absence of ripening heat or light in the summer'. He also remarked that it was one of the tallest magnolias he had seen.

In cultivation it grows into a tall, erect shrub or small tree to about 30ft (9m). It is commonly known as the Glossy Magnolia on account of its beautiful oval foliage, which is up to 4½in (11cm) long and 2in (5cm) wide. In an article entitled 'Chinese Magnolias in Cultivation' (1950), George Johnstone wrote:

> It has the most lovely foliage, the leaves being more highly polished than any evergreen leaf that I know of – better than the best Hollies. The young growth is bronze, also very highly polished. The leaf has a silver edge to it. If you hold it up, so that the sun is behind it, you will see that silver edge all the way round each leaf.

Magnolia nitida takes about 15 years to flower from seed. The flowers are fragrant, ivory or cream coloured, to 3in (7.5cm) across, and appear during March and April on shoot tips. The best forms are those of a pale primrose-yellow colour with a purple streak down the outer tepals. The seed is also particularly attractive, being a beautiful shade of orange.

In the British Isles *M. nitida* is hardy only in localities which provide it with adequate shelter and frost protection – it has been grown successfully in a few gardens in Cornwall and at Ventnor on the Isle of Wight. It is probably to be regarded as hardiness zone 9, although there have been recent reports of plants having survived temperatures of 10°F (−12°C) (zone 7/8).

A rich, moisture-retentive, preferably acid soil in dapple shade would suit this rare species.

Magnolia officinalis

This fast-growing, medium-sized tree is known almost entirely from cultivated plants in the Chinese provinces of Hupeh and Szechwan.

It was first discovered by Augustine Henry, an Irishman who went to China as a medical officer and Assistant Inspector of Customs in 1881. He became interested in plants because one of his assignments was to compile a report on the drug plants used by the Chinese. This started a correspondence with the Royal Botanic Gardens at Kew which led to a number of important plant discoveries and introductions, including *Magnolia officinalis*, which he found growing in eastern Szechwan in 1885. It was introduced into cultivation by Ernest Wilson in 1900 when he was on a Veitch expedition to western Hupeh and later, when he was collecting for the Arnold Arboretum, from areas to the north and south of Ichang, an important town on the Yangtze river.

It is rare in cultivation in the British Isles, where *M. officinalis* var. *biloba* is more commonly seen. The type may be restricted to Cornish gardens as it was often confused with the closely related *M. hypoleuca*, differing by its pubescent young shoots (glabrous in *M. hypoleuca*), yellowish-grey young wood (purple-brown in *M. hypoleuca*), and flat-topped fruit (cone-shaped in *M. hypoleuca*).

The leaves are obovate in shape to 18in (46cm) in length by 8in (20cm) in width, green above and slightly glaucous beneath. The underside is also covered with fine down, especially noticeable on the midrib. The leaves tend to be concentrated towards the end of the branchlets (as in *M. hypoleuca*), producing a ruff-like effect, and are rather papery in texture. The creamy white flowers are produced on leafy shoots, are cup-shaped, about 6in (15cm) across, and quite fragrant, with a rather antiseptic scent. In the British Isles they are seen during June (May in China and North America), but are not produced in sufficient quantity to be regarded as a visual attraction.

The fruiting cones are about 5in (7.5cm) long, flat-topped, and generally oblong in shape. They are red in colour but quickly turn a dull purple-brown.

The Chinese know this species as the Hou-po or Hou-phu Tree and grow it extensively for its bark and flower buds, which have prized medicinal qualities. The bark when boiled yields an extract which is taken internally as a cure for coughs and colds and as a tonic and stimulant during convalescence. An extract obtained from the flower buds, which are called Yu-po, is esteemed as a medicine for women. Once the bark has been stripped, the tree dies – which probably accounts for its disappearance from its native habitats.

The more commonly seen *M. o.* var. *biloba* was first described by Ernest Wilson in 1927 in Kiangsi Province but was introduced into cultivation by Sir Harold Hillier from seed or scions received from the Lu-Shan Botanical Gardens in 1936. It is a fast-growing, medium-to-large tree of an upright stature that puts on about 18in (46cm) of growth per year in favoured locations. Trees in the Hillier Gardens and Arboretum are 30ft (9m) in height by 12ft (3.5m) across after some 30 years. The leaf is of a similar size, shape, and character to that of the type, but is distinct in that it has a deep notch at the tip, which gives it a bilobed appearance. This character comes true when plants are raised by seed. In cultivation it grows in similar situations to *M. hypoleuca*, in a rich, moisture-retentive, acid soil in a sunny site sheltered from strong winds. In North America it has been reported as growing successfully in Michigan, which indicates a similar hardiness rating to *M. hypoleuca* (US hardiness zone 5).

Magnolia salicifolia

Magnolia salicifolia (see page 84), the Japanese Willow Leaf Magnolia, varies in habit from an erect, large shrub to a broad, spreading, medium-sized tree. It is found growing in oak and beech forests at moderate elevations – between 2,000ft (600m) and 3,000ft (900m) – on the Japanese islands of Honshu, Shikoku, and Kyushu.

It was introduced almost simultaneously to North America (in 1892) and to the British Isles (in 1893) by Professor C. S. Sargent, Director of the Arnold Arboretum, and the English nurseryman James Harry Veitch. Both were collecting in Japan, on Mount Hakkoda on northern Honshu, and both sent back quantities of seed to their respective establishments. Sargent's seed germinated, Veitch's did not. However Veitch obtained seedlings a year later from Sargent, presumably from this same source. The Yokohama Nursery Company sent a plant from a different source to Kew in 1906.

The tree forms are generally upright in growth becoming pyramidal in shape, increasing by up to 2ft (60cm) per year. They can be single or multi-stemmed and will reach 50ft (15m) or more in sheltered environments in the south of England. The 'Mount Hakkoda' form is a much broader crown tree with large flowers which open about two weeks later than those of the type. This was formerly referred to as *M. salicifolia* var. *concolor*. A fastigiate multi-stemmed form was described by J. G. Millais in *Magnolias* as *M. salicifolia* var. *fastigiata*; this appears similar in growth, habit, and flower size to 'Wada's Memory' (see page 127). 'Jermyns', a large-flowering, slow-growing, ultimately large shrub, completes the range.

The foliage of *M. salicifolia* gives off a most distinctive scent. The leaves and young shoots, when crushed, smell of aniseed. The leaves are oblong lanceolate or elliptic in shape and up to 5½in (14cm) in length and 2in (5cm) in width. They are green above and glaucous green below.

The fragrant, pure-white flowers open during early April on slender leafless stems from an early age. They generally consist of six tepals which are held horizontally and tend to nod over as they open fully to 4in (10cm) or 5in (12.5cm) across. The fruiting cones are small and cylindrical in shape, to 3in (7.5cm) in length. They are bright rose-pink in early October but soon fade to a dull brown.

M. salicifolia prefers to be grown in a moisture-retentive, acid soil and in the British Isles can be grown in full sun or dappled shade. It is quite hardy and in North America is rated to hardiness zone 5.

M. × *proctoriana*, 'Kewensis', and 'Wada's Memory' all have *M. salicifolia* as a parent. Stephen Spongberg in his *Magnoliaceae Hardy in Temperate North America*, published in 1976, regards *M. salicifolia* as a species variable enough to be able to accommodate these 'hybrids' (for which see pages 123, 127) under its species name.

Magnolia sargentiana

Sargent's Magnolia develops into a large tree of an upright habit and is native to the Chinese provinces of Yunnan and Szechwan. The species was first discovered in 1869 by Armand David, a French missionary and naturalist, near the area of Mupin in western Szechwan. Ernest Wilson rediscovered it later, in 1903, and first collected seed in 1908. He found it growing in thickets and moist woods on and to the west of Wa-shan in western Szechwan between 5,000ft (1,500m) and 6,500ft (2,000m). He sent it to the Arnold Arboretum, Boston, where it was first raised in 1909. It was named after Professor Charles Sprague Sargent, the Director of the Arboretum.

Over the next few years a number of Wilson's Chinese Magnolias were introduced to the Arnold Arboretum, but problems arose in keeping young plants alive, especially during the severe winters often experienced in eastern North America. Professor Sargent decided to ship all these young plants to Chenault's Nurseries at Orleans to be propagated. In a letter of 3 July 1913 to Léon Chenault, he proposed 'To send to you this autumn the entire stock of these plants with the understanding that you will propagate them as largely as possible and then after you have got up a stock of them, return to us a couple of plants of each species, reserving others for yourself'. Sargent's gamble paid off. Plant introduction records from the Royal Botanic Gardens, Kew, show that Chenault must have distributed a plant of *M. sargentiana* immediately after receiving the consignment from the Arnold Arboretum. He also distributed grafted plants to Kew in 1918.

M. sargentiana grows very large. Wilson reported seeing a tree 80ft (24m) tall whose trunk 6ft (1.8m) from the ground was 10ft (3m) in girth and was clean for 16ft (5m) before the branches commenced. The branches were very numerous and wide spreading, forming a massive head of flattened-oval contour. In the southwest and south of England large rather spindly and twiggy trees of 50ft (15m) or more can be found; these will be in the region of 40 years of age.

The glossy green leaves are extremely variable in shape and up to 7in (18cm) long by 4in (10cm) wide. They are generally obovate and are rounded or occasionally notched at the apex. The underside is a grey-green in colour and is covered with downy hairs.

The flowers are slightly frost tender as they tend to shed their protective perules during the autumn and winter. The 12 tepals are a deep pink colour on the outside and a pale pink inside. The 8in (20cm) flowers, which open during late March and April, are held in a variety of positions – upright, horizontal, or slightly nodding. They have a subtle, almost medicinal fragrance. Seedlings take up to 25 years before they start to flower but budded plants will be flowering between 10 and 15 years. The fruiting cones are cylindrical, between 4in (10cm) and 5in (12.5cm) in length, and initially a dark red colour.

M. sargentiana prefers a sunny site in association with other woodland plants and needs a moist, humus-rich, acid soil. It is quite hardy, despite its exotic appearance, roughly equating with US hardiness zone 7. Both the plant and the flowers are surprisingly wind tolerant.

M. sargentiana var. *robusta* (see page 52) is sufficiently distinct to merit individual attention. Ernest Wilson saw this plant in fruit but not in flower during his fourth and last expedition to China in 1910. He discovered it on the Wa-shan in western Szechwan, some 30 miles to the east of where he collected *M. sargentiana*, growing at an altitude of 7,600ft (2,300m). It was one of the plants that Sargent handed over to Chenault for propagation.

To a horticulturist's eye, *M. s.* var. *robusta* is more closely allied to *M. dawsoniana*, which is found some 80 miles to the west of Wa-Shan, at Tatsien-lu in western Szechwan.

In cultivation in the south and southwest of England *M. s.* var. *robusta* forms a wide, spreading, bushy tree to about 40ft (12m) in height and as much in width, with branching occurring a few feet above ground level.

The leaves – generally found at the end of the shoots – are variable, being obovate to ovate and sometimes elliptic, with many having a distinctive notch at the apex. In size they measure up to 8in (20cm) in length by 3½in (9cm) in width. The flowers are seen in large numbers, the sickle-shaped buds opening out to reveal beautiful flowers up to 12in (30cm) across with 12 to 16 rose-purple tepals. (Flowers do vary from pale pink to purple.) They open in a near-horizontal position but as they unfold bend over to present their full faces. They are slightly fragrant, with a scent that has been likened to that of wintergreen. They flower from a comparatively early age, even if seedling raised, with upwards of 11 years being cited. A mature specimen in full flower, with the sheer weight of blooms bowing down the branchlets, is one of the most spectacular of flowering trees. The fruits are larger and more prolific than those of *M. sargentiana*, being oblong in shape up to 8in (20cm) in length. It is similar in hardiness to *M. sargentiana*.

M. s. var. *robusta* is the parent of a number of fine floriferous hybrids. Examples that are well worth growing are: 'Princess Margaret' and 'Michael Rosse' (both of them *M. campbellii* var. *alba* × *M. s.* var. *robusta*);'Caerhays Belle' (*M. s.* var. *robusta* × *sprengeri* 'Diva'), a beautiful, broad-tepalled, pale-pink flowered hybrid raised at Caerhays Castle in 1951; and 'Mark Jury' (*M. campbellii* subsp. *mollicomata* 'Lanarth' group × *M. s.* var. *robusta*), a fine hybrid with 10in (25cm) purple flowers that was raised in New Zealand.

Magnolia sieboldii

This large, broad, spreading shrub (see page 87) is native over a wide geographic area, being found in the forests of Japan on the Islands of Honshu, Shikoku, and Kyushu and in Korea, south Manchuria, and the Chinese provinces of

Anhwei and Kwangsi. Mr Arthur deCarle Sowerby collected the species in southern Manchuria, where it grew in stream valleys throughout the hills surrounding Shenyang. Ernest Wilson also found it, in 1918, in the forests of Korea. He reported that 'it delights in rocky, granite country and is specially happy by the side of forest streams. On the Diamond Mountains in northeast Korea, where the winter temperature is more severe than in Massachusetts, this lovely Magnolia is a feature, and I have hopes of this Korean form being a better garden plant than the Japanese one now in cultivation'.

It is thought to have been introduced into the British Isles first to Veitch's Coombe Wood Nurseries somewhere between 1879 and 1888 and then to the Royal Botanic Gardens at Kew in 1893.

It is a large shrub of a broad, spreading habit. Given ideal conditions (a moisture-retentive acid loam in semi-shade) it will grow quite vigorously. J. G. Millais cites a plant in his garden in Sussex that measured 22ft (6.7m) by 21ft (6.4m) across within 15 years. In less favourable locations up to 12in (30cm) of growth per year may be expected, with plants reaching 6ft (1.8m) by 6ft (1.8m) after 10 years.

The leaves are oblong in shape, to 6in (15cm) long by 3½in (9cm) wide, and are glaucous green and downy beneath. The sheer beauty of the species is to be found in the nodding flowers, which are held sufficiently stiffly to 'look you in the face', and are most prolific from early June onwards. The flowers still show during late June and early July and again in early August. They are probably the purest white of all the magnolia flowers. The nine tepals, up to 4in (10cm) across, contrast most vividly with the ring of stamens, which vary in colour from a red to a deep crimson, the latter thought to be from Wilson's Korean introduction of 1918. The flowers are fragrant, especially at dusk. Plants flower young, at five years old.

Small pink fruiting cones, 3in (7.5cm) long, can be seen during late September.

M. sieboldii is the parent of two particularly interesting hybrids, 'Charles Coates' (*M. sieboldii* × *M. tripetala*) (see page 120) and *M.* × *wieseneri* (*M. hypoleuca* × *M. sieboldii*) (see page 127).

There has been some doubt over the hardiness of this species, with instances of dieback being reported. From my experience, it is quite hardy in the British Isles when planted in suitable sites. Temperatures of 1.4°F (−17°C) (zone 6/7) have not caused dieback. This has been substantiated in North America, where temperatures as low as 9°F (−23°C) have been quoted. *M. sieboldii* has also been recommended as the most suitable magnolia for cultivation in Scandinavia. Here mature specimens have been known to withstand a temperature of −39°C (−38°F), with the ground frozen to a depth of 3ft (90cm), for a period as long as a week. Even under these most extreme of conditions, the plants seemed to suffer no adverse effects; they flowered quite happily in the following August.

Opinions vary as to the soil type preferred by *M. sieboldii*; it has been said to be a lime-hater but has also been said to be reasonably tolerant of lime. Provided that a moisture-retentive soil is provided and a sheltered semi-shaded site chosen, I see no reason why it will not grow in alkaline conditions, although it will flourish more freely in acid soil.

Magnolia sinensis

This attractive broad, spreading shrub (see page 86) is native to the Chinese province of western Szechwan, where Ernest Wilson first discovered it growing 'amongst miscellaneous broad leaved deciduous trees and shrubs, Rhododendrons and silver firs at an elevation from 7,000 to 9,000ft on and around the moist woodlands of the Wa-Shan'. It was one of the Chinese Magnolias distributed by Professor Sargent to Léon Chenault for propagation (see page 114) and it arrived in the British Isles via Chenault's Nursery in 1920.

In cultivation *Magnolia sinensis* grows into a rather straggly shrub to 20ft (6m) high and as much across. It puts on 12in (30cm) to 18in (46cm) of growth per year. The bark is a distinctive fawn colour. The leaves are obovate in shape and rounded at the apex. They measure up to 7in (18cm) long by 5in (13cm) wide and have a distinctive coating of silky hairs on the underside.

The fragrant flowers are fully pendant, up to 5in (7.5cm) across, and composed of nine tepals. In the British Isles they appear, on leafy shoots, in late May and early June and produce a secondary flush in August. The visual appeal of the flowers is enhanced, as it is in *M. sieboldii*, by the dramatic colour contrast of the white tepals with the ring of crimson stamens. The fruiting cones are 3in (7.5cm) in length, pendant, and at first pale pink, although they turn to brown as they age.

M. sinensis is at home in either acid or alkaline soil, as long as it is moisture retentive and mulched regularly. Many regard it as being best sited in full sun, but although this may be so in areas of high rainfall or of high atmospheric humidity, dappled shade certainly suits it better in areas of low rainfall or of high summer temperatures coupled with high light levels. It is rated as US hardiness zone 6.

Magnolia sprengeri

Two distinct forms of *Magnolia sprengeri* are grown today – the pink-flowered 'Diva' and the white-flowered *M. sprengeri* var. *elongata*.

'Diva' was a single plant raised from a batch of seeds sown at Veitch's Coombe Wood Nursery under the collection number of Wilson 688 (all the other seedlings turned out to be the white-flowering form *M. s.* var. *elongata*). The seeds came from plants found by Ernest Wilson in September 1901 growing in moist woodland south of Ichang, near Chan'yang Hsien in Hupeh. Wilson at first thought that what he had found was the wild type of *M. denudata*, but the fact that his discovery had flowers with 12 tepals (against the 9 of *M. denudata*) showed that it was truly *M. sprengeri*. 'Diva' develops into a broad, spreading tree that can reach 50ft (15.25m) in height in southwest England and have a spread in excess of 30ft (9m). The green leaves, which unfurl as the last flowers start to fall, are obovate in shape, nearly 7in (18cm) long by 4½in (11.5cm) wide, and are quite hairy, especially on the midrib on the underside of the leaf. The slightly fragrant 8in (20cm) flowers appear during April and are a beautiful rosy pink on the outside and pale pink streaked with darker lines on the inside. The flowers are saucer-shaped and the tepals have a tendency to curl upwards and inwards at the tip. The flowers are prolifically produced and borne almost down to ground level. The original plant took 19 years to flower from seed, but grafted plants can be expected to flower in 12 to 15 years. Budded plants on *M.* × *soulangiana* stock have flowered when they have reached a height of 7ft (2m).

'Diva' flourishes in a moisture-retentive acid soil, in a sunny yet sheltered site. In the United States it is highly regarded because of its hardiness – it is reported to have withstood temperatures of −18°F (−27.8°C) in Michigan, which equates to US hardiness zone 5.

'Diva' has produced a number of attractive seedlings which are regarded as the same species although they differ in flower colour. 'Claret Cup' (see page 55), 'Copeland Court' and 'Eric Savill' (see page 54) are noteworthy examples. It is also a parent of 'Caerhays Belle' (*M. sargentiana* var. *robusta* × 'Diva'), 'Galaxy', and 'Spectrum' (both *M. liliiflora* 'Nigra' × 'Diva'), all of which are worthy of planting.

'Galaxy' and 'Spectrum' (see page 50) have been raised and named by the United States National Arboretum. Both cultivars have tulip-shaped, purple-pink to red flowers, borne in the same way as those of *M. l.* 'Nigra', in a succession of flushes from mid-April onwards, but larger. 'Spectrum' is a broad, spreading, large shrub while 'Galaxy' is a fast-growing smaller (potentially medium-sized) tree. Both flower within five years of raising and are regarded as US hardiness zone 5.

M. s. var. *elongata* differs from 'Diva' in a number of ways. It is less vigorous, developing into a small multi-stemmed tree of between 20ft (6m) and 30ft (9m), dependent on site, with obovate leaves to 4½in (11.5cm) long and 2¼in (5.7cm) wide. The flowers have white or creamy white tepals which can be flushed with purple at the base; they are delicately held, opening like miniature water lilies.

Although overshadowed by its more flamboyant sister, *M. s.* var. *elongata* should not be overlooked – it is well suited to areas where space is limited.

Stephen Spongberg in his *Botanical Revision of Hardy Magnolias* agrees that the white form is properly called *M. s.* var. *elongata*, but refers to the pink form as *M. s.* var. *sprengeri* and reserves the name *M. s.* var. *sprengeri* 'Diva' for a plant grown by J. C. Williams of Caerhays Castle.

Magnolia stellata

This, the Star Magnolia (see page 72), is the best known of all magnolia species. It is a slow-growing, rather densely branched shrub (or, occasionally, small tree) which has been cultivated in Japan for centuries. It is native to the mountains of southern Honshu in the Prefecture of Gifu in Chupa District. Trees of 22ft (6.7m) have been reported here, but it is uncertain whether these are native or originally of cultivated origin. They grow in sphagnum bogs with *Alnus hirsuta* and *Ilex crenata*.

The first confirmed introduction into Western gardens was made by Dr George Hall of Rhode Island, New York, who, in 1861, brought this species and *Magnolia kobus* back and passed them on to the Parsons Brothers, nurserymen of Flushing, New York, for propagation. It is uncertain when or by whom *M. stellata* was introduced into the British Isles. John Gould Veitch and Richard Oldham are reported to have sent plants back in the early 1860s, but more probably it was Charles Maries, the English plant collector, who introduced it (again along with *M. kobus*) in 1877 or 1878.

In cultivation it forms a dense, twiggy shrub which will ultimately reach 20ft (6m) in height. Plants at the Hillier Gardens and Arboretum are 10ft (3m) in height by 12ft (3.7m) across after 20 years. Growth varies, depending upon the selection and the method of propagation – grafted plants increase at a faster rate than plants produced by cuttings. Young rooted cuttings once established will increase by approximately 12in (30cm) per year.

The green leaves are elliptic to obovate in shape, measuring 4in (10cm) long by 2in (5cm) wide. As this species has been cultivated by the Japanese for centuries, a wide diversity of flower size, number of tepals, and colour can be expected. Faintly fragrant flowers open in succession, on leafless stems, over a number of weeks from late March to early May, depending on site, situation, and selection. Individual flowers vary in size between 3in (7.5cm) and 4in (10cm) across, although a vigorous American selection has produced flowers that can reach as much as 5in (12.5cm) across. The number of tepals varies enormously – it can be anything from 12 to 40. The colour is generally white or creamy white, though a number of forms have a pink flush, especially when the flower first opens. The plants flower at only 18 months old.

M. stellata needs a moisture-retentive soil in a sunny position if flowering is to reach its potential. It does best in acid soils but will grow in alkaline soils provided regular mulching is carried out in the autumn or spring. It is quite hardy, being regarded as US hardiness zone 5. Some forms have a still greater frost tolerance – 'Royal Star', for example, is reported to have withstood temperatures as low as −35°F (−37.2°C).

'Centennial' is an American selection raised at the Arnold Arboretum and named during the Arboretum's centennial year (1972). It is similar to the British 'Water Lily', with up to 32 tepals. It is a vigorous-growing plant.

'Dawn', an American selection popularized by Harold Hopkins of Maryland in the 1970s, is described as a good pink with up to 45 tepals on mature plants. Plants in the British Isles do not conform to this description, either in colour or tepal number, but this may well be because they are as yet too young.

'Rubra', probably of Japanese origin, produces, when mature, carmine-pink 4in (10cm) flowers with up to 15 narrow tepals. The colour is deeper than that of 'Rosea', 'Rosea King', or 'Rosea Massey' (sometimes known as 'Dr Massey'), and a dark pink bar runs longitudinally along the back of each tepal. Older plants – those over 20 years old – have a tendency to develop a more open-branched framework than do *M. stellata*'s white-flowered forms.

'Norman Gould' is a colchicine-induced form raised at the Royal Horticultural Society's Garden at Wisley in the early 1950s. It is very slow growing – the original plant is still, after 35 years, only about 17ft (5m) high. Extremely floriferous, it bears from an early age large snow-white flowers up to 6in (15cm) across on leafless stems. The tepals are broad and comparatively few.

Neil Treseder in his *Magnolias* describes three distinct American selections of *M. stellata* that bear the name 'Waterlily'. Each is vigorous, carries pink-flushed flowers with over 30 tepals, and flowers between one and two weeks later than other forms of *M. stellata*. They are all quite distinct from the clone 'Water Lily' in cultivation in the British Isles (see page 73), which has no trace of pink in the flower.

M. stellata has been hybridized with the closely related Japanese species, *M. kobus* to produce *M.* × *loebneri* (see page 123), with *M. liliiflora* to produce the de Vos and Kosar hybrids (see page 120), and with *M. salicifolia* to produce *M.* × *proctoriana* (see page 124).

For the purpose of this book, the nomenclature *M. stellata* and *M.* × *loebneri* has been retained, but some authorities would disagree with this. Stephen Spongberg in *Magnoliaceae Hardy in Temperate North America* suggested that *M. stellata* should be regarded as a variety of *M. kobus* and should therefore be named *M. k.* var. *stellata*. *M.* × *loebneri* should, similarly, be referred to as *M. k.* var. *loebneri*. Other botanists consider that *M. stellata* should now be called *M. tomentosa*, claiming this to be the oldest published name for this species.

Magnolia tripetala

The Umbrella Magnolia (see page 56) is a small-to-medium tree found in the deep rich forests of eastern North America – in the Allegheny Region from Pennsylvania southward through the Appalachian and Ozark Mountain ranges, to Florida, Arkansas, and Missouri. It occurs in moist soils high in humus and is mainly found in protected ravines, along streams, and on lower mountain slopes to an altitude of 2,200ft (650m). It grows in association with many hardwoods, including *Liquidambar styraciflua* (Sweet Gum), *Acer rubrum* (Red Maple), *Liriodendron tulipifera* (Tulip Tree or Yellow Poplar), and *Betula lenta* (Sweet or Cherry Birch). It was first introduced into the British Isles in 1752, probably in one of John Bartram's consignments to Peter Collinson, who is believed to have first flowered this species at Mill Hill, London, on 24 May 1760.

It is an upright-growing tree, seldom exceeding 40ft (12m) in its native habitat, often multi-stemmed, with upright shoots radiating from the base. In the British Isles it is vigorous, with between 2ft (60cm) and 3ft (90cm) of growth commonly seen on established plants. The green leaves, of a thick papery texture, are among the largest in the genus, being up to 20in (50cm) long and 10in (25cm) wide; they are of an obovate lanceolate shape tapering to the apex and the base. It gets its common name, Umbrella Tree, from the way in which the leaves cluster towards the end of branches. The creamy-coloured flowers are vase-shaped and in the British Isles appear on the ends of leafy shoots during late May and early June. They have between 9 and 16 tepals (usually 12) and when open are up to 8in (20cm) across. They are seen rather sporadically, which may not be a disadvantage – this is one of the few magnolia species with a disagreeable smell to its flowers. It will take about eight years from seed before flowers can be seen. The conical fruiting cones are about 4in (10cm) long. Their bright red colour makes them probably the most attractively fruited of the American species grown in the British Isles.

Despite its tropical appearance it is extremely hardy – hardiness zone 4 in North America. It requires a sunny yet sheltered site and a humus-rich and moisture-retentive soil. The bark may be chewed like tobacco and is said to be a cure for smoking.

Two forms have been selected: 'Bloomfield' for its large flowers, which are reported to be of dinner-plate size, and for its leaves, which measure 28in (70cm) long by 12in (30cm) wide; and 'Woodlawn', for its large fruiting cones, which are 5in (12.5cm) by 2in (5cm) and still bright red.

M. tripetala is a parent of a number of hybrids, including 'Charles Coates' (*M. sieboldii* × *M. tripetala*), *M.* × *thompsoniana* (*M. tripetala* × *M. virginiana*), and 'Silver Parasol' (*M. hypoleuca* × *M. tripetala*). 'Silver Parasol' is so named because of its silvery bark and the parasol arrangement of its foliage. It has inherited the fine scent and large flowers – up to 10in (25cm) across – of *M. hypoleuca*.

Magnolia virginiana

The Sweet Bay Magnolia is found over an extremely wide geographic range in the coastal plain and Piedmont regions of eastern North America, between Massachusetts and New York, in Georgia and Florida and in Texas, Arkansas, and Tennessee. With such a wide distribution it varies considerably in habit from a large multi-stemmed deciduous shrub in northern locations to a large evergreen tree of 60ft (18m) or more in favoured locations in the south. The sites vary from wet, sandy, often acid soils along streams, swamps, and flatwoods to moist, rich, deep soils. As trees, they are found in association with *Acer rubrum* (Red Maple), *Persea borbonia* (Red Bay), and *Gordonia lasianthus* (the Loblolly Bay).

The Sweet Bay was the first magnolia to be introduced into the British Isles; it is known to have been grown in Bishop Compton's garden at Fulham Palace in 1688 (see page 11).

In cultivation in the British Isles it is not a particularly strong grower and is generally seen as a straggly shrub increasing slowly each year. Some good specimens have been seen, notably at the University of Cambridge Botanic Gardens, where a specimen in excess of 30ft (9m) has been grown. A range of forms has been tried here, but none has been entirely successful – to make really strong growth *Magnolia virginiana* seems to need the hot, ripening summers of eastern North America.

The oblong-to-oval leaves are up to 5in (12.5cm) long by 2in (5cm) wide; they are pale green above and glaucous white and quite downy beneath. (This characteristic accounted for one of the species' original names, *M. glauca*.) The flowers have a rich fragrance, once described as 'one of the best outdoor scents – cool and fruity and sweet', but, in the British Isles at least, they make little visual impact. They are small, up to 3in (7.5cm) across, with eight creamy white tepals which green with age but last for two days only. In its native habitats *M. virginiana* flowers from June until mid-August; in the British Isles, even in southern climes, it flowers rather sporadically during August and September. Fruiting cones are seldom seen in the British Isles but in North America they are an ornamental feature, being crimson in colour with bright red seeds.

In the British Isles a wide range of soils, provided they are moisture-retentive and not hot and dry on the one extreme or waterlogged on the other, can sustain *M. virginiana*. A sunny yet sheltered site is desirable. The northern deciduous forms are quite hardy, being regarded as US hardiness zone 5. There is an evergreen clone called 'Milton' growing in Boston, Massachusetts, which is 30ft (9m) high, columnar in habit, and about 30 years old. This is also reported to be zone 5.

M. virginiana has been hybridized with a number of species. Noteworthy among the hybrids produced are *M.* × *thompsoniana* (*M. tripetala* × *M. virginiana*) (see page 126), 'Freeman', and 'Maryland' (*M. grandiflora* × *M. virginiana*) (see page 121). It has also been crossed with *M. macrophylla* (and flowered in the 1987 clone 'Karl Flinck') and with *M. fraseri*.

Magnolia wilsonii

Wilson's Magnolia (see page 86), named after its finder, Ernest Wilson, is a broad, spreading, large shrub that comes from the Chinese Provinces of eastern Kansu, western Szechwan, and northern Yunnan. Of its habitat, Wilson wrote:

> This Magnolia is quite a common shrub in the woods of western Szechwan, especially around the town of Tachien-Lu. It is found at elevations between 7,000ft and 8,500ft on the edge of woods in thickets and more especially along mountain streams, growing with deciduous trees and shrubs, Rhododendrons, Silver Fir, Spruce and hemlock Fir. Usually it is a straggling bush anywhere from 10 to 15ft tall and as much through.... It was discovered by me in the summer of 1904 and introduced into English gardens by seeds which I sent to Messrs Veitch in the autumn of that year.

These seeds must have failed to germinate, for it was a further 16 years before *Magnolia wilsonii* was introduced into the British Isles. It was collected again by Wilson in 1908, this time for the Arnold Arboretum, which in turn distributed plants to Léon Chenault (see page 114).

In cultivation it develops into a multi-stemmed large shrub, but if judicious pruning is carried out from the beginning it is possible to grow it as a single-stemmed small tree up to 20ft (6m) in height. A specimen at the Hillier Gardens and Arboretum is 18ft (5.5m) high by 18ft (5.5m) across after 23 years and makes up to 2ft (60cm) of growth per year. *M. wilsonii* can be distinguished at any time of the year by its very dark brown branchlets, which appear almost black after the first year of growth. The leaves are generally elliptic to lanceolate in shape and up to 7in (18cm) long by 4in (10cm) wide. The leaves are quite downy on the underside and initially pale brown, although they later take on a silvery appearance.

The fragrant flowers open to a cup shape during May and June and are about 4in (10cm) across. Each flower consists of nine pure white tepals with a ring of rich rose-red stamens (not quite as stunning a combination as *M. sieboldii*) and are often seen (like *M. sinensis*) producing a secondary flush in August. In western North America, with its higher prevailing temperatures, flowering takes place earlier, in March and April, and the blooms are often larger, up to 6in (15cm) across. The fruiting cones are cylindrical in shape and up to 4in (10cm) long; they are pinkish during early October and gradually fade to a dirty brown by mid-November.

M. wilsonii prefers a sheltered semi-shaded site and a moisture-retentive soil, which may be on either the alkaline or the acid side of neutral. In North America it is regarded as hardiness zone 3.

M. × *highdownensis* was given to the late Sir Frederick Stern as a pan of unlabelled seedlings by J. C. Williams of Caerhays Castle in Cornwall. When it first flowered it was considered to be a hybrid between *M. sinensis* and *M. wilsonii*. Stephen Spongberg, however, regards it as *M. wilsonii*, because it is similar to specimens of the species collected in China and it falls into the range of variation encountered in cultivation of the species.

Magnolia Hybrids

'Charles Coates'
This multi-stemmed large shrub or small tree (see page 68) arose as a chance seedling in the Azalea Garden of the Royal Botanic Gardens, Kew, around 1946. Mr C. F. Coates, the propagator in charge of the Arboretum nursery, identified it as a distinct, self-sown seedling and it was named in his honour.

It is regarded as a hybrid between *Magnolia tripetala* and *M. sieboldii*. The main stems are strongly ascendent, while the lateral branches give a broad, spreading effect. Plants at the Hillier Gardens and Arboretum are 30ft (9m) in height by 20ft (6m) across after 25 years of growth. The leaves resemble those of *M. tripetala*, even to the extent of congregating on the ends of the shoots. The papery green leaves are broadly elliptic in shape, 10½in (27cm) long by 5¾in (14.5cm) wide, and are a glaucous green on the underside with distinctive hairs along the midrib. The very fragrant flowers resemble those of *M. sieboldii* but instead of nodding they are held erect; they are saucer-shaped, to 7in (18cm) across. The eight tepals are creamy white in colour and have a distinctive red ring of stamens which can be seen during late May and June.

It prefers an acidic moisture-retentive soil and a sheltered site in dappled shade. In the southeast of England young leaves have a tendency to scorch if they are exposed to strong direct sunlight, but this may not be the case in areas where light intensity or temperature are not so great, or, perhaps more significantly, where atmospheric humidity levels are greater. It is quite hardy, being regarded as suitable for US hardiness zone 6.

The de Vos and Kosar Hybrids
In April 1965, eight new magnolia cultivars were formally named by the US National Arboretum. They had resulted from a breeding programme carried out 10 years before by Dr Francis de Vos, Arboretum Geneticist, and William Kosar, Arboretum Horticulturist. Pollen from *Magnolia stellata* 'Rosea' was transferred to *M. liliiflora* 'Nigra' to produce six of the eight hybrids; 'Rosea' pollen with *M. liliiflora* 'Reflorescens' and *M. stellata* 'Waterlily' pollen with 'Reflorescens' produced the remaining two.

All are multi-stemmed, rounded or conical in habit and of an erect growth pattern to about 15ft (4.6m) in height, dependent on cultivar. The leaves vary between ovate to elliptic in shape, averaging 6in (15cm) long by 3in (7.5cm) wide. The flower buds show colour and open just before the leaves appear in early May, continuing on leafy shoots into June; they are generally not worried by late spring frosts. The fragrant flowers are held upright and are either cup-shaped or saucer-shaped. They vary in colour from pink through to purple. In North America all these cultivars flower about three weeks earlier, seem more vigorous and have a more intense flower colour than plants grown in the British Isles. This better performance is probably due to the fact that the North American plants enjoy more favourable summer temperatures and light conditions than do their British cousins. In plants grown in both the British Isles and North America the flower colour and number of tepals appear to vary from year to year, which may perhaps be due to environmental conditions. All prefer an open, sunny site and a moisture-retentive, acid soil.

The hybrids are listed here in order of flowering. The time of flowering and colour of flowers refers to plants in eastern North America. Their parentage is *M. liliiflora* 'Nigra' × *M. stellata* 'Rosea' unless otherwise stated.

'Anne'
Flowering begins on this erect-growing plant during mid-April. The erect flowers up to 4in (10cm) across are red-purple in colour on both sides of the eight tepals.

'Betty'
The flowers, produced in mid- to late April, are very large, up to 8in (20cm) across, and have up to 19 tepals; they are red-purple on the outside and white on the inside. This is a vigorous grower.

'Judy'
The candle-like flowers open during late April; they are small, up to 3in (7.5cm) across. The 10 tepals are red purple on the outside and creamy white on the inside. This is a slow-growing plant of a fastigiate habit.

'Randy'
A very floriferous hybrid, flowering during late April, with flowers up to 5in (12.5cm) across. The buds, initially held erect, are red-purple externally and white inside; up to 11 tepals splay out on opening. 'Randy' is an erect grower with an almost columnar habit.

'Ricky'
The red-purple flowers open during late April and are up to 6in (15cm) across; the 15 tepals are often twisted. It is a vigorous grower of an erect habit.

'Susan'
A compact grower; the fragrant flowers open during late April and have six red-purple tepals.

'Jane' (*M. liliiflora* 'Reflorescens' × *M. stellata* 'Waterlily')
This cultivar is distinguished by its beautifully shaped, very fragrant flowers, red purple on the outside and white on the inside, which open in early May. There are 10 tepals which measure 4in (10cm) across. 'Jane' is a strong, vigorous grower with an upright habit.

'Pinkie' (*M. liliiflora* 'Reflorescens' × *M. stellata* 'Rosea')
'Pinkie', a plant of compact, rounded habit, is the latest of these hybrids to flower – in mid-May – and has the palest flowers. They are white inside and pale red-purple outside, up to 7in (18cm) across, and have 12 tepals.

The Freeman Hybrids
Oliver Freeman of the United States National Arboretum, Washington, D.C., pollinated *Magnolia virginiana* with *M. grandiflora* during 1931. Two years later a number of young plants were lined out in nursery rows; they started to flower some six years from sowing.

Two plants were selected and named as 'Freeman' (see page 62) and 'Maryland'. 'Maryland' develops into a multi-stemmed large shrub in the British Isles or a small tree in North America. The leaves are similar to those of *M. grandiflora*, being evergreen, oblong lanceolate in shape, to $8\frac{1}{2}$in (22cm) long by $3\frac{1}{2}$in (9cm) wide, and with undulating margins. The lemon-scented flowers are slightly larger than those of 'Freeman', open more widely to a distinctive cup-shape, and are seen during July and August in the British Isles (May and June and a second flush in August in North America). Both 'Freeman' and 'Maryland' flower from an early age, inheriting this attribute from *M. virginiana*. They take after *M. grandiflora* in being adaptable as far as sites and soils are concerned, although they prefer a hot, sunny site in a moisture-retentive soil.

'Maryland' and 'Freeman' have both remained unscathed when temperatures have dropped to 7°F (−14°C) (US hardiness zone 7) in the southeast of England. Temperatures have been slightly more severe than this at Windsor, where plants have also been unscathed since they were planted in the early 1960s.

'George Henry Kern'
This medium-sized deciduous shrub was raised in 1935 by Carl E. Kern of Wyoming Nurseries of Cincinatti, Ohio, and named after the nursery's owner, Carl E. Kern, who was killed on active duty in 1945 while serving in the United States naval reserve.

It was originally thought to be a hybrid between *Magnolia* × *soulangiana* and *Magnolia stellata*, but it is now considered to be *M. liliiflora* 'Nigra' × *M. stellata* 'Rosea'.

In growth, 'George Henry Kern' resembles *M. stellata* – it increases by about 12in (30cm) per year – but it is quite distinctive in flower colour and time of flowering. The flowers are composed of between eight and ten strap-shaped, thick-textured tepals and are rose-pink in bud opening to a light pink. The flowering period is exceptional, starting on leafless shoots in mid- to late April and continuing into early July, when the plant is in full leaf. In North America the colour seems intensified, being a deep reddish-purple in bud, opening to a rose pink on the outer surface and a pale pink on the inner surface.

'George Henry Kern' prefers a sunny situation in a moisture-retentive, acid soil. Hardiness zone 5.

The Gresham Hybrids
During the mid-1950s, the late Drury Todd Gresham embarked on a massive magnolia hybridization programme, the rewards of which are still being reaped.

It is worthwhile recording Gresham's philosophy as he saw it:

> It is not too great a stretch of the imagination to envisage Magnolias of the future, and their spectacular appeal for the modern gardener. They will bloom quickly from seed or graft; under Californian conditions maiden blooms from seed may be expected in 4 to 5 years; blossoms will be larger, to 12 and 14in, of heavy substance, wide variation in form, and increased tepals; pure colour, tints and shades of warm pink, pink salmon, rose, true reds, red violet, blue violet, yellow apricot, orange and scarlet;

novelty combinations of colour and colour pattern; trees will be aborescent, vigorous in growth, and better branching habit; foliage ornamental, showing plum red and foxy red spring colouring with less tendency to chlorosis; stature dwarf or treelike to suit any conceivable garden situation.

The Journal of the Royal Horticultural Society, 89 (1964), 'Deciduous Magnolias of Californian Origin'

When Gresham first considered this hybridization programme, the pure vibrant colours of *Magnolia campbellii* attracted him, but the extra hardiness, the colour purity, and time taken to bloom of one of its progeny, *M.* × *veitchii*, led him to select this. He crossed it, and a second generation plant, *M.* × *veitchii* 'Rubra', with *M.* × *soulangiana* 'Lennei Alba' and *M. liliiflora* 'Nigra' to produce his 'Svelte Brunettes' and 'Buxom Nordic Blondes'.

The Svelte Brunettes are strong-growing, small-to-medium trees, all with strong, ascending branch frameworks and all very floriferous, with a honey scent to the bloom. In southern England they flower during late April and early May, predominantly on leafless stems, after many of the damaging frosts have passed; in California, where they were first raised, they flower from late February onwards. Six cultivars resulting from the *M. liliiflora* 'Nigra' × *M.* × *veitchii* cross were named in 1961. A check of the parental influences shows that *M. campbellii* contributed the 12 tepals, of which 8 reflex at maturity and 4 remain upright. *M.* × *veitchii* has contributed the high-standing bud and *M. liliiflora* the depth of colour often found in the tepals. 'Heaven Scent' (see page 92) has heavily flushed, dark pink or rose-purple tepals. 'Peppermint Stick' (white flowers heavily flushed with dark pink), 'Dark Raiments' (red-violet flowers), and 'Raspberry Ice' (large lavender-pink flowers) are other examples worthy of cultivation.

The Buxom Nordic Blondes are also vigorous small-to-medium trees which may spread with age. Plants in the Hillier Gardens and Arboretum are 18ft (5.5m) in height after 18 years, but young vigorous plants in other collections in southern England are growing at a rate of between 2ft (60cm) and 3ft (90cm) per year and flower four years from planting. The flowers differ from those of the Svelte Brunettes – they are milk white but flushed with a delicate shade of pink at the base of the tepals. Ten cultivars have been named. 'Sayonara' (see page 93), with globular, white, pink-flushed flowers to 7in (18cm) to 8in (20cm) across, is a first-class garden plant. In warmer growing conditions, it will produce flowers 12in (30cm) across. 'Sulphur Cockatoo' has large, fragrant, white flowers, the inner six tepals being stained with violet pink at the base. 'Rouged Alabaster' bears white flowers flushed with clear pink.

Todd Gresham also used a wider range of seed and pollen parents – *M. campbellii*, *M. campbellii* var. *mollicomata*, the cultivars 'Maharajah', 'Maharanee', and 'Charles Raffill', *M. sargentiana* var. *robusta*, *M. dawsoniana*, *M. sprengeri* 'Diva', *M.* × *veitchii* and 'Rubra', *M. liliiflora* 'Nigra', the best *M.* × *soulangiana* varieties, and even second-generation Gresham hybrids have all been used to produce a multitude of seedlings.

Shortly after Gresham's death in 1969 some 10,000 of his young hybrids were transferred to the Tom Dodd Nurseries in Alabama and 1,600 larger plants were sent to the Gloster Arboretum in Mississippi for further evaluation. From these crosses the next generations of Gresham hybrids are now becoming available commercially; nine were released in the mid-1980s.

'Tina Durio' (*M.* × *veitchii* × *M.* × *soulangiana* 'Lennei Alba') is one of the most popular hybrids in North America; 'huge 10 to 12in pure white fragrant flowers are borne in profusion on this vigorous fast growing tree. The heavy textured white "sculptured" blossoms are broad tepalled and open up wide to create a showy bloom covered tree at the height of the long bloom season which is late enough in the spring to escape freeze damage'. 'Elisa Oldenwald' is of similar parentage but is multi-stemmed in habit.

'Darrell Dean', 'Joe McDaniel', 'Peter Smithers', and 'Todd Gresham' are all *M.* × *veitchii* × *M.* × *soulangiana* 'Rustica Rubra' crosses. They are all fast-growing trees with large goblet- or bowl-shaped fragrant flowers which in Louisiana open wide to 10in (25cm) to 12in (30cm) across. Flower colour varies from a deep pink, through violet-rose, to a dark wine-red colour.

'Mary Nell' (*M. soulangiana* 'Lennei Alba' × *M.* × *veitchii* 'Peter Veitch') has cup-shaped thick-textured flowers, up to 10in (25cm) across, which are white but stained purple-red at the base of the tepals. It is late to flower in spring and takes after *M.* × *soulangiana* in habit.

David Ellis of Magnolia Nursery and Display Gardens in Alabama offered six more Gresham hybrids in 1988. They vary from fast-growing trees to trees of compact habit. 'Sangreal' is described as a vigorous-growing tree and an outstanding and easily noticeable performer at flowering time, with cup-shaped red-purple flowers which are longer lasting than most. 'Jon Jon' is reported to be late flowering, almost in a season by itself, with large red-purple flowers. 'Pink Goblet' is an early to mid season flowerer with the classical goblet-shaped, pink to red-purple flowers. Other cultivars include 'Dark Shadow', 'Full Eclipse', 'Wine Light', and 'Candy Cane'.

The full impact of the Greshams outside North America is not fully appreciated. The first generation Greshams (the Svelte Brunettes and the Buxom Nordic Blondes) are only now becoming popular in the British Isles so it will be sometime before the later cultivars can be fully evaluated in Britain. Of the Greshams that I have grown, noticeable attributes are their prolific flowering qualities from an early age, their vigorous upright habit when young (they may well spread with age), and their lateness of flowering (from late April onwards).

They are quite hardy, being tested to US hardiness zone 6, will grow well in full sun or dappled shade, and prefer a moisture-retentive, acid soil.

Magnolia fanciers will have to 'watch this space' in specialist nurserymen's lists for some time to come to appreciate the full value of Drury Todd Gresham's work. However, despite the varied breeding programme, care will be necessary to ensure that many of the new varieties do not simply duplicate what has already been achieved.

'Kewensis'

This broad, spreading, small-to-medium tree (see page 80) first arose as a chance seedling at the Royal Botanic Gardens, Kew, in 1938. It was discovered by Mr C. F. Coates, propagator in charge of the Arboretum Nursery. It was described and named in 1952, when it was considered to be intermediate in both floral and foliage characters between two Japanese species, *Magnolia salicifolia* and *M. kobus*.

It grows vigorously, upright initially but spreading to form a broad spreading tree. A tree at the Hillier Gardens and Arboretum measures 35ft (11m) by 20ft (6m) after 25 years of growth. Established plants increase by about 18in (45cm) per year. The green leaves are oblong lanceolate to elliptic in shape, 5in (12.5cm) long by 2¼in (6cm) wide, and closely resemble those of *M. salicifolia*, although they do not have the distinctive strong aniseed scent of that species. The young stems when rubbed do however have a lemon-verbena scent. The fragrant, pure white flowers open during mid- to late April on leafless stems. The six tepals are held horizontally and when fully out are slightly nodding; they are about 4in (10cm) to 5in (12.5cm) across and are borne unfailingly and abundantly each year. Plants will flower well from an early age.

'Kewensis' grows best in a sunny site in a moisture-retentive preferably, acid soil. It is regarded as being perfectly hardy (US hardiness zone 5).

Botanical opinion believes that this 'hybrid' should be regarded as a clone of *M. salicifolia*.

Magnolia × loebneri

Loebner's Magnolia is a hybrid that quickly develops into a dainty single or multi-stemmed small tree or large shrub. The early work of hybridizing *Magnolia kobus* with *M. stellata* was done in Germany prior to 1914. Five plants were in 1923 sold by Loebner to Wilhelm Kordes, who owned a nursery at Sparrieshoop in Germany. Kordes in turn sold the plants at a later date to Hillier Nurseries of Winchester, and so introduced this hybrid into the British Isles. Similar deliberate hybridization programmes have taken place in North America, notably at the Arnold Arboretum and the University of Illinois, with fragrant, very floriferous cultivars resulting. Chance hybrids have also appeared in established European gardens.

A diversity of habits has resulted, ranging between single-stemmed ultimately broad-crowned trees to 30ft (9m) and multi-stemmed large shrubs. Growth rates vary too, but may be 20in (50cm) per year on established plants. The leaves are similar in size to those of *M. stellata*, 5in (12.5cm) long by 2in (5cm) wide, elliptic to oblong, and a slightly lighter green beneath. The flowers are seen most abundantly from an early age, with hardly a bare branch to be seen on mature plants. They vary in size, from 4½in (11.5cm) to 6in (15cm) across; colour, from pure white to a lilac-purple; and number of tepals, from 8 to 30. In the British Isles they are seen at their best during the second half of April and stand up well to late frosts. In North America they generally open slightly earlier, though plants in the southern States have been known to open as early as January.

All are remarkably tolerant of a wide range of soil types, from acid to alkaline and from a light sand to a moisture-retentive (but not waterlogged) clay. They will flower in dappled shade but are best in full sun. They are surprisingly wind resistant and quite hardy (US hardiness zone 5).

Stephen Spongberg regards *M. stellata* as a variety of *M. kobus*. As *M. × loebneri* is regarded as a hybrid between these two species, *M. × loebneri* should now be classified as a variety of *M. kobus*.

'Ballerina'

This was raised by Professor Joe McDaniel at the University of Illinois during the 1960s. It develops into a small tree increasing by about 12in (30cm) to 15in (38cm) of growth each year. It is one of the last of the group to flower. The fragrant flowers are white with a pale pink flush towards the base of the tepals, of which there may be as many as 30.

'Merrill'

Probably the most vigorous of all, 'Merrill' (see page 77) develops into a broad, spreading tree which in North America exceeds 30ft (9m) in height by as much across. Plants at the Hillier Gardens and Arboretum are about 20ft (6m) in height after 20 years. Pure white flowers, 4in (10cm) to 6in (15cm) across, with up to 15 broad tepals, are seen in profusion during late April.

'Leonard Messel'

The least vigorous clone, 'Leonard Messel' (see page 76) develops a more crowded framework than the others. The flowers, 5in (12.5cm) across and composed of up to 12 strap-shaped tepals, appear in April and are quite frost resistant. This clone is probably the darkest pink in colour of any *M. × loebneri* in cultivation in the United States and Canada.

'Neil McEacharn'

This was raised at the gardens at Windsor Great Park from seed of *M. stellata* 'Rosea' sent from the garden of Captain Neil McEacharn at Villa Taranto on Lake Como, Italy. Plants at the Hillier Gardens and Arboretum are 15ft (4.5m) in height by 10ft (3m) across after 15 years; they bear white multi-tepalled flowers to 4in (10cm) across.

Magnolia × proctoriana

This small tree (see page 82) of pyramidal outline arose as a selected seedling from a batch of *Magnolia salicifolia* seed sent to the Arnold Arboretum in 1928 by Mr T. R. Proctor, who had opened a private arboretum at Topsfield, Massachusetts. It was described and named in 1939 when it was considered to be intermediate between two Japanese species, *M. salicifolia* and *M. stellata*.

In habit, it grows into a broad, spreading, small tree with slender, ascending shoots. Trees at the Hillier Gardens and Arboretum are 25ft (7.5m) in height by 20ft (6m) across after 20 years. Trees of this size put on between 15in (38cm) and 25in (63cm) of growth per year.

The leaves are similar to those of *M. salicifolia*, being oblong lanceloate in shape, 5in (12.5cm) long by 1¾in (4.5cm) wide, and a paler green beneath. The leaves when crushed are scented but not nearly to the same degree as those of *M. salicifolia*. The abundant flowers open during mid- to late April on leafless stems. They are white with a hint of pink at the base of the tepals, which are generally six in number but do vary up to twelve. The slightly fragrant blooms open horizontally to 4in (10cm) across and tend to nod once they are fully open.

Closely related to this is *M. × proctoriana* 'Slavins Snowy', which was raised at Highland Park, Rochester, New York. This develops into a small tree of an upright habit that flowers profusely at the same time as *M. × proctoriana*, but has fragrant, slightly larger flowers to 6in (15cm) across, with a distinctive pink blotch at the base of each of the six to nine tepals.

M. × proctoriana is considered by Spongberg to be a variant of *M. salicifolia*, and is therefore subsumed under that name. All the examples I have seen of *M. × proctoriana*, however, show a distinctive habit not normally encountered in *M. salicifolia*.

A rich, acidic, moisture-retentive soil in full sun ideally suits this plant, but it will flower well in the semi-shade when planted in gardens in southern England. Allow plenty of space for this broad, spreading tree to flourish. It is cited as US hardiness zone 5.

Magnolia × soulangiana

This muli-stemmed large shrub or broad, spreading, small tree (see pages 33, 36, 38) is probably the best known and most widely planted of all magnolias; it is the archetypal magnolia.

The story of its raising and introduction by Etienne Soulange-Bodin is recorded on page 11. This was the start of a continuous story of cultivar introductions through to the present day by plant hybridizers in Europe, Japan, New Zealand, and North America, all of whom raised plants to suit their own tastes and climatic conditions, so that by the 1980s there are over 100 named cultivars of this hybrid. Hybridizers have also produced a range of interesting second-generation hybrids, produced back crosses with *Magnolia liliiflora* 'Nigra', and made crosses with other species and hybrids – most noticeably with *M. × veitchii* (see Gresham hybrids, page 121) – to produce plants in keeping with modern trends.

The leaves are quite variable, being broadly elliptic to obovate in shape, up to 8in (20cm) long by 4½in (11.5cm) wide, dark green (often glossy) above and paler beneath with fine hairs along the midrib. The flowers open on leafless stems but may be seen at the same time as the unfurling leaves. In the British Isles, this has been noticed when a particularly late warm spring has followed a long cold winter. When this happens the beauty of the floral spectacle is considerably impaired. April and early May is the normal time for flowering in southern England, although it is earlier in the United States. The flowers vary considerably in size, shape and colour, and are generally goblet-, cup- or saucer-shaped. The nine tepals can be white, pink, or purple or variously streaked on the outer and inner surfaces and can be as large as 10in (25cm) across.

Any but thin, dry, chalky soils are suitable for these plants, although a deep, moisture-retentive, slightly acid soil which can be fed at regular intervals with quantities of organic matter or inorganic fertilizer will suit them best. A sunny site is essential if effective flowering is to occur. Dependent on cultivar, they are regarded as being between the maximum and minimum ranges of US hardiness zone 5.

'Alexandrina'

This was originally introduced by Cels of Montrouge, Paris, in 1831, but it appears to have been mixed over the years and the name covers an assortment of clones. The French clone, which has nine tepals, flowers a week after the flowering peak of the *soulangiana* group. The flower is fragrant, tulip-shaped, 4in (10cm) long, white flushed with purple on the outside and white inside. Another erect form recognized under this name produces pure white flowers which are slightly larger, up to $4\frac{1}{2}$in (11.5cm) long. These two are considered to be probably the hardiest of all the 'Alexandrina' clones.

Japanese nurseryman in Alabama and Louisiana coastal areas introduced a plant to the local nursery trade as *M.* × 'Alexandrina' in about the late 1920s. In Mobile, Biloxi, and New Orleans it is often called the Japanese Magnolia. The pink-purple flowers, white inside, bloom ten days later than the trade form *soulangiana* and are lasting and fragrant. 'Alexandrina' is safe in zone 4.

'Brozzonii'
A late-flowering hybrid raised at the gardens of Camillo Brozzoni at Brescia, Italy, during the latter part of the 19th century, 'Brozzonii' was distributed by French nurserymen early in the 20th century. It is a vigorous grower bearing white flowers, made up of six $5\frac{1}{2}$in (14cm) long tepals, which on full opening are up to 10in (25cm) across.

'Burgundy'
A floriferous, early-flowering hybrid raised by W. B. Clarke of San Jose in 1930, this was introduced into the British Isles in the 1960s. The flowers are rose-pink in colour and open to 8in (20cm) across. In North America, where light conditions differ from the British Isles, the flowers are a deep purple-red that better justifies the cultivar name.

'Dark Splendor'
This is an American cultivar producing a compact, floriferous hybrid with wine-red flowers. It is the result of a back cross, carried out in the 1960s, of *M.* × *soulangiana* 'Rustica Rubra' with *M. liliiflora* 'Nigra'.

'Just Jean'
This floriferous hybrid resulted as a chance seedling found by John Gallagher in Dorset, England, during the 1970s. It has a compact habit and distinctive, large, obovate foliage. During the middle of April it produces clear pink, goblet-shaped flowers flushed deep pink at the base.

'Lennei', 'Lennei Alba'
'Lennei' is a fast-growing, free-flowering, small-to-medium tree. Very large, pink, cup-shaped flowers are produced on plants which are only four years old from cuttings. It has been used (as a seed parent) to raise 'Iolanthe' (*M.* × *soulangiana* 'Lennei' × 'Mark Jury'). 'Iolanthe' was raised by Felix M. Jury at Waitara, North Island, New Zealand. It is considered to be US hardiness zone 5 to 6. 'Lennei Alba' has been used by Todd Gresham, who crossed it with M. × *veitchii* 'Rubra' to produce the range of fascinating hybrids described on page 121.

'Picture'
'Picture' (see page 35) has been used by Pickard's Magnolia Gardens, Kent, England, to produce an interesting range of second-generation hybrids from which vigorous, fragrant large-flowered hybrids of erect growth were selected. Many produce goblet-shaped flowers, which open up from 9in (23cm) to 12in (30cm) across, with deep wine-red tepals. Good light conditions are essential for these plants to grow successfully. Results in other parts of the British Isles have not matched the success seen in Kent, but spectacular results have been seen in southeast Switzerland (Morocote near Lugano, the home of Sir Peter Smithers). Of the 13 or so named cultivars the following are good (given the correct growing conditions); 'Pickard's Ruby' (with wine red to purple flowers), 'Pickard's Garnet' (deep wine red), and 'Pickard's Charm' (pink). 'Picture' has also been crossed with *M. sprengeri* 'Diva' to produce an American hybrid that is being named 'Big Dude'. It is thought to have an improved hardiness rating.

'Rustica Rubra'
(See page 34)

'San Jose'
The flower description on page 39 refers to the plant in the Henry F. Dupont Garden and to plants in cultivation in the British Isles distributed by the Crown Estate Commissioners at Windsor Great Park. However, Philip J. Savage Junior refers to a plant bearing the same name but with a different description being in cultivation in North America. 'The entire bloom is a pure marble white, except for a striking "thumb print" of dark pink almost red at the very base of each tepal'. Both cultivars are from W. B. Clarke's Nursery of San Jose and have probably been mixed since they were raised in the 1930s, so it is impossible now to know which is the 'correct' description.

'E. Soulange-Bodin'
The type plant of *M.* × *soulangiana* introduced by M. Soulange-Bodin merits conservation, not only on historical grounds but also for its floristic merits. The flowers are a beautiful warm pink colour on the outer surfaces (rosy red in bud) and white with a faint flushing of pink on the outside of the broad tepals.

'Sundew'

This cultivar was introduced in 1966 by Pickard's Magnolia Gardens and is a second-generation 'Picture' seedling with fragrant creamy-white flowers, which can have a hint of orange-pink.

'Verbanica'

This is a cultivar of French origin – it was raised by Leroy of Angers in 1873. The cup-shaped flowers are an attractive rich clean pink fading to white at the tips of the tepals. 'Verbanica' is probably one of the last cultivars of *M.* × *soulangiana* to flower in May. When cultivated well it produces an attractive display of well-spaced clean pink flowers, but when it is starved or badly sited the flowers are smaller and more crowded and have a distinctive 'dirty pink' colour.

Magnolia × thompsoniana

This wide-spreading large shrub is a hybrid between two American magnolias, *Magnolia virginiana* and *M. tripetala*. It first arose in the nursery of Archibald Thompson in London in 1808, which makes it the first magnolia hybrid to have arisen in the western world, pre-dating *M.* × *soulangiana* by about 12 years. One theory is that a seedling was selected from a batch of imported seed sown by Thompson. Another, which takes into account the fact that *M. tripetala* had been cultivated in the London area for about 50 years, is that seed from a plant of *M. virginiana* grown by Thompson was sown, germinated, and selected on site. There is evidence to support both theories, but when the plant was first featured in *Curtis's Botanical Magazine* of 1820 it was not considered to be a hybrid at all, merely a large-leaved form of the American Sweet Bay, *M. virginiana*. It was not until 1876 that the Dutch Botanist C. de Vos confirmed its current status, which has more recently been supported by Professor Joe McDaniel. In the 1960s, he carried out deliberate cross pollinations between the two suspected parents and produced plants that conformed almost exactly to the description originally given in *Curtis's Botanical Magazine* in 1820.

It grows into a rather ungainly shrub up to 20ft (6m) in height by 15ft (4.5m) across in the southeast of England, though larger in milder habitats and in the southern United States. The leaves are very variable in size, but up to 9in (23cm) long by 4in (10cm) wide. They are generally elliptic in shape, often with undulating margins, and are glossy green in colour above and a glaucous to silvery green beneath, with fine hairs coating the entire undersurface. In most parts of the British Isles it is deciduous, losing its leaves late in November or December. In mild localities or in the southern United States it is semi-evergreen.

In the British Isles the flowers are creamy white to primrose-yellow; they are borne sporadically, on leafy shoots, from May through to July and August. They are quite fragrant (a quality inherited from *M. virginiana*), vase-shaped, and up to 4in (10cm) long and 5in (12.5cm) across.

It is a plant that deserves to be more widely distributed because of the attractiveness of its foliage and of its flowers, which are seen from an early age and over a long period. It needs a hot, sunny, yet sheltered site and space to spread. It is quite hardy, being quoted as US hardiness zone 6, however exposure to −25°F (−31.7°C) in the United States has been recorded. Young plants 3ft (90cm) high and one year from planting survived temperatures of 10°F (−12°C) in southern England without damage, which is a fair indicator of their hardiness rating.

Magnolia × veitchii

This fast-growing tree was first raised in Exeter at the Royal Nurseries of Peter C. M. Veitch in 1907. Veitch's objective was to raise a hybrid which was 'as beautiful as its parents, more hardy and that would flower in a reasonable time'. According to the late Mr W. T. Andrews, Veitch's nursery manager, pollen was taken from *Magnolia denudata* and other kinds and transferred on to a free-flowering *M. campbellii* which was growing at the New North Road nursery site. (Mr J. G. Millais in 1927 and Mr J. E. Dandy in 1950 report the cross as being the other way round). Six seedlings resulted, only two of which were retained – 'Peter Veitch' (see page 91), with pink flowers, and 'Isca' (the Roman name for Exeter), with white flowers, pale pink in bud.

Both grow into medium-to-large trees. 'Peter Veitch' is more vigorous and upright than 'Isca', which has a distinctly broader spreading habit. Young trees can increase in growth by more than 3ft (90cm) per year. Both have a reputation for casting limbs during high winds. This is particularly so with 'Peter Veitch' because it is a heavy-limbed tree, often multi-stemmed, with congested branches. A tree growing at Caerhays Castle in Cornwall was found to be over 90ft (27.5m) in height when measured in 1984, making it the tallest tree magnolia in the British Isles. (It was planted in 1921.)

The green leaves are obovate or oblong in shape, to 12in (30cm) in length and 7in (18cm) in width, with a distinctive point at the apex. When they first unfurl they have a purplish tinge, especially on the underside, which quickly disappears as the leaf increases in size. The fine grey down is found on the underside along the midrib and partially along the main veins.

'Peter Veitch' is the cultivar normally encountered. Its flowers are pink, chalice-shaped, have 9 tepals, are up to 6in

(12.5cm) long, and are seen on leafless branches in mid-April. It is a most prolific-flowering tree and reliably so.

'Isca' has pure-white flowers which are smaller and less prolifically produced than those of 'Peter Veitch'. 'Isca' is said to open a week before 'Peter Veitch' in Devon and Cornwall, but specimens in the Hillier Gardens and Arboretum open more or less on the same day. Both cultivars take from seven to ten years before they start to flower reliably.

A sunny yet sheltered site is needed for these vigorous growers, which require moisture-retentive soil, preferably on the acid side of neutral. They are regarded as US hardiness zone 7.

M. × *veitchii* 'Rubra' was raised by James S. Clarke, nurseryman of San Jose, California. It is similar in all respects to 'Peter Veitch' except for the flower, which is a wine-red colour when in bud. Another quality is that it flowers from an early age. It is also hardier, being US hardiness zone 6. *M.* × *veitchii* has been used by hybridizers as a parent of the 'Gresham' hybrids (see page 121).

'Wada's Memory'

This small tree (see page 81) of a compact upright habit was named by the University of Washington Arboretum, Seattle, when it was selected from a batch of seedlings received in March 1940 from Japan. The Director of the Arboretum, Brian Mulligan, records:

> *Magnolia kobus* 'Wada's Memory' was one out of a number of plants of this species purchased from the nursery of K. Wada, Numazushi, Japan. Undoubtedly they were all seedlings, since most of the progeny have very ordinary flowers, typical of *Magnolia kobus*. This one however, which by chance was placed in a very prominent position in the Arboretum, has flowers about twice the size of the normal type (6 to 7in wide when expanded, but the segments soon reflexing or drooping).

An interesting fact about the naming of this plant is that it was named in honour of Koichiro Wada while he was still alive.

It is a free-growing, multi-stemmed small tree retaining a compact conical habit. A tree in the Hillier Gardens and Arboretum is about 22ft (6.7m) in height by 12ft (3.7m) across after approximately 20 years. The green leaves are elliptic in shape, 5in (12.5cm) long by $2\frac{1}{4}$in (5.75cm) wide. The unfurling leaves are a distinctive mahogany red, a colour which disappears as they mature. The fragrant flowers are borne on leafless stems during late April in such profusion that they present the viewer with a glistening white pyramid of flower. The six tepals are at first held horizontally, but within a day of opening they increase in size and droop as if the flower was past its best. This effect is quite startling, when on a sunny cloudless day a gentle breeze causes the tepals to dance like butterflies hovering over a flower prior to collecting nectar.

Its value as a garden plant is increased because it flowers from an early age. A sunny yet sheltered site should be chosen and it should be planted in moisture-retentive soil which can be either side of the neutral line. It is quoted as US hardiness zone 5.

Some botanical authorities regard 'Wada's Memory' as a natural hybrid between *M. kobus* and *M. salicifolia*, while others consider it to be a clone of *M. salicifolia* itself. Whatever it is, it is indeed a most distinctive tree that merits attention.

Magnolia × wieseneri

This deliciously scented, multi-stemmed, large shrub or broad, spreading, small tree (see page 89) is a hybrid between two Japanese species, *Magnolia hypoleuca*, which has a wide distribution from Hokkaido in the north to the Ryukyu Islands in the south, and *M. sieboldii* from Honshu, Shikoku, and Kyushu. It is unlikely that it is a hybrid that has occurred naturally in the wild. Magnolia species generally protect themselves against natural hybridization by occupying different habitats and by flowering at slightly different periods. In the artificial surroundings of a garden landscape, however, these natural defences are broken down. So it is probable that this hybrid occurred spontaneously or by design in Japanese gardens during the 19th century or before.

It was on the Japanese stand at the Paris Exposition of 1889 that it first appeared in Europe. Many admired it, including W. J. Bean, who acquired a specimen for the Royal Botanic Gardens, Kew. It was described some two years later by Joseph Hooker (later Sir Joseph), Director of Kew, who named it *M.* × *watsonii* after W. Watson, an Assistant Curator at Kew. Unknown to Hooker, another plant has been purchased at the Exposition by M. Wiesener, a local landowner, after whom the hybrid was named by Carriere when he described it in 1890, some six months before Hooker. Under the Rules of the International Code of Botanical Nomenclature, the earlier name takes priority.

The habit of *M.* × *wieseneri* is midway between its two parents; it is a multi-stemmed large shrub or small bushy tree to 20ft (6m) in height. A plant in the Hillier Gardens and Arboretum is 18ft (5.5m) in height by 15ft (4.5m) across after 20 years. It is a strong, upright grower when young, increasing by up to 2ft (60cm) per year, but with age the crown shape will spread. The leaves are obovate in shape and quite leathery in texture, approximately 8in (20cm) in length by $4\frac{1}{4}$in (10.5cm) in width. They are green above and a glaucous green beneath and covered with fine down, which is most prominently seen on the midrib and main veins.

The plant is mainly grown for the scent of its flowers, which has been variously described as ethereal, medicinal, spicy, aromatic, and like pineapples. On the first day of opening the upward-facing flowers are cup-shaped, 4in (10cm) to 5in (12.5cm) across, with up to nine ivory-white tepals. On opening the central boss of deep red stamens is revealed, creating an eyecatching combination of colour. The globular shape is maintained for a few days (dependent on the levels of insect pollinators present), then the flower splays out to 7in (15cm) to 8in (20cm) across and loses some of its appeal. The plant starts to flower from a fairly early age, the flowers appearing rather sporadically from mid-June and lasting for about a month.

When it was first introduced into cultivation it had the reputation of being slow and difficult to grow, but this was presumably because only poorly grafted specimens were then available. With modern propagation techniques it is not uncommon for a plant to attain a height of 5ft (1.5m) 15 months after budding. It is quite hardy in the British Isles and is rated as US hardiness zone 5. It does, however, need a sheltered site in dappled shade to give of its best, when it rewards its grower by offering a delicious fragrance on a warm, still summer's evening. It is not widely distributed even in specialist collections, a fact that needs to be remedied. Perhaps because I have not seen many specimens, I have seen this plant only growing on acid soils, either on well-drained, sandy soil where regular top dressings are carried or on a heavy, loamy (but not waterlogged) clay, on both of which it gives a good account of itself.

Like many magnolia hybrids, this magnolia produces little or no seed in its true form. Its pollen is fertile, however, and for Philip Savage in Michigan it has produced interesting hybrids with *M. tripetala* 'Bloomfield', *M. virginiana* (northern form), and one of its parents, *M. hypoleuca*.

The Magnolia's Cousins

The family Magnoliaceae is divided into two subfamilies or tribes, Magnolieae and Liriodendreae. Within the Magnolieae the only genera sometimes encountered apart from *Magnolia* itself are *Manglietia*, *Michelia*, and *Talauma* while in Liriodendreae there is only one genus, *Liriodendron*.

Manglietia

Manglietia (the name is a latinized adaptation of the Malaysian word for a native species) is a small genus of evergreen plants that have from four to six seeds per carpel, as against the magnolia's two. There are about 25 species, which are found in the eastern Himalayas, across southern China, and southwards through Thailand, Cambodia, Vietnam, and Laos to Malaysia, Sumatra, and Java.

The majority of the species are tropical in distribution, although according to J. E. Dandy, in *A Survey of the Genus Magnolia together with Manglietia and Michelia*, five species are of temperate origin. *Manglietia duclouxii* from northeast Yunnan and *M. szechuanica* from western Szechwan have never been introduced into cultivation. Three species – *Manglietia forrestii* (from western and southern Yunnan), *M. hookeri* (from western Yunnan, also Upper Burma), and *M. insignis* (from western Yunnan) – have, however, been introduced by George Forrest.

Manglietias are seldom seen in cultivation. Apart from a few gardens in southwest England, where they grow reasonably successfully, they can be found only in collections of temperate plants under glass such as at the Royal Botanic Gardens of Edinburgh (*M. hookeri* Forrest 27364) and at Kew (*M. insignis*). They are also cultivated in the warm temperate climates of the southern states of North America.

Manglietia insignis

M. insignis is most commonly seen of the three cultivated species. It also has the widest natural distribution, coming from the Himalayas, eastward to central China as far as southwest Hunan and northern Kwangsi, and northern Vietnam. George Forrest collected the species, but Reginald Farrer also saw it, in Upper Burma when he visited Hpimaw during 1919:

> We [E. H. M. Cox and he] discovered a new magnolia-like tree from our veranda .... It was a noble evergreen about thirty feet in height with glossy dark green leaves, which we have noticed vaguely before and wondered if it produced anything that could be called a flower. And here it was pushing a long purple bud under our noses, a bud that graced the point of every twig and opened into a glorious salmon pink chalice. The petals never expanded to the extent of the usual platter-shaped magnolia, but held their graceful curve until they withered ... a plant to dream about.

In Yunnan George Forrest found it growing to heights of 90ft (27.5m) at altitudes between 3,000ft (900m) and 4,500ft (1,350m). In cultivation it is a multi-stemmed small tree from 25ft (7.5m) to 30ft (9m) in height. The leathery, glossy green leaves are up to 10½in (26.5cm) long by 4in (10cm) wide and are oblanceolate in shape and slightly glaucous beneath. The flowers have been described as fragrant, with 9 to 12 tepals which vary in colour from a white to a creamy yellow often with a tint of pink or purple. The oblong fruiting cones are up to 5in (7.5in) long and purple red when ripe.

M. insignis is too tender to have widespread appeal, but in the southwest of England, at Caerhays Castle in particular, it can be seen as a multi-stemmed small tree between 25ft (7.5m) and 30ft (9m) high. It is regarded as US hardiness zone 9. It prefers to be grown in moisture-retentive, acid soil in dappled sunlight, but it can succeed in full sun where moisture and humidity levels are high.

Two or more fine young trees of this species have been growing for 30 years in the Strybing Arboretum in Golden Gate Park in San Francisco, California, along with the big trees of *M. campbellii* that thrive there.

Manglietia fordiana

M. fordiana, a native of Hong Kong, is another species occasionally met with in cultivation. Surprisingly, a young plant at the Hillier Gardens and Arboretum has survived outside since 1983 (temperatures to 10°F, −12°C) and is now 4ft (1.25m) in height. Here, though, it is not really warm enough for it to succeed; it flourishes more in the states of North America, where it is sold commercially.

Manglietia fordiana has been collected in the vicinity of Hwang Shan, in Anhwei province, China, by Ren Chang Ching. There are specimens in the herbarium of the Chicago Museum of Natural History and at Grays Herbarium at Harvard University.

Michelia

Michelia, named in honour of Pietro Antonio Micheli (1679–1737), a Florentine botanist, is a genus of evergreen plants differing from *Magnolia* and *Manglietia* primarily by having its flowers in clusters, both in the axils of its leaves and terminally at the shoot tips. There are about 45 species, extending from India and Sri Lanka eastwards to Japan and southwards to Malaysia, Sumatra, and Java.

The majority of the species are tropical, however a few can be grown in mild regions of the British Isles, southern Europe bordering onto the Mediterranean, and the southern states of North America.

Michelia doltsopa

M. doltsopa is probably the best known of the temperate species grown. It is found in Nepal eastwards into western Yunnan and was introduced into the British Isles by George Forrest in 1918. When it is grown in the southern states of North America, it develops into a small-to-medium, pyramid-shaped tree to 40ft (12m) in height. In sheltered gardens in the southwest of England and southern Ireland it grows as a large multi-stemmed shrub to 20ft (6m) in height and as much across. Its glossy, green, leathery leaves measure up to 7in (18cm) long by 3in (7.5cm) wide, although they are considerably longer in North America, where they are reported to reach 12in (30cm). The very fragrant flowers, which vary from a pale yellow to white in colour, are up to 4in (10cm) across and usually appear in April (January to April in the southern states of North America). During warm spells they are profusely produced. Each flower consists of 12 to 16 tepals. The silky-rust-coloured bracts that surround the flowers present in their own right a visually attractive display.

A moisture-retentive soil in a sunny site sheltered from strong winds is advised for this species. It is proving hardier than initially thought, being quoted as hardiness zone 8 in North America.

Michelia figo

This species (see page 96) from southeastern China is more at home in the warm south-facing gardens of the French and Italian Rivieras, where it grows as a large multi-stemmed shrub to 20ft (6m) in height. The leathery leaves are narrowly oval in shape and 4in (10cm) long by 2in (5cm) wide. The flowers, creamy yellow edged with purple and up to 1½in (4cm) across, are extremely fragrant, which makes up for their rather insignificant appearance. 'Port Wine', a Japanese cultivar, is reported to have pink flowers. 'Stubbs Purple' has purplish flowers.

Michelia × foggii

Michelia × foggii is an American hybrid between *M. doltsopa* and *M. figo* that produces fragrant flowers, 3in (7.5cm) long, which are white or white with a deep pink picotee edging. It is considered to be hardy in the southern states. A selection is reported to become deciduous at −12°C (10.4°F), but to leaf out in the spring.

Michelia compressa

M. compressa is the hardiest species to be grown in the British Isles, being native to the mountains of southern Japan, Taiwan, and the Ryuku Islands. Ernest Wilson saw this species when he visited the island of Taiwan in 1918. He found it growing in dense forest on steep slopes near Musha in central Taiwan. In the wild it is reported to grow to 40ft (12m) and to have a compact rounded habit. A plant in the Hillier Gardens and Arboretum – in a sheltered location in dappled shade – has grown strongly, developing into an upright, single-stemmed, small tree. The glossy leaves are 4in (10cm) in length by 1½in (3.75cm) in width and the small, rather insignificant, pale yellow flowers up to 1in (2.5cm) across.

A number of Chinese species have recently been introduced into North America, where they are grown in the southern states. They include *M. bodinieri*, which is also represented in the Hillier Gardens and Arboretum; *M. maudiae*, which has large, cup-shaped, fragrant white flowers to 5in (12.5cm) across; *M. wilsonii*, which has ivory white flowers; and *M. yunnanensis*, whose cup-shaped 2in (5cm) wide flowers are white flushed with scarlet. These species grow alongside *M. velutina*, a plant from Nepal and Sikkim with 4in (10cm) long fragrant straw-coloured blooms, which has been in cultivation in the West since 1855.

Talauma

Talauma, thought to be derived from an indigenous name of the West Indian species, is a genus of evergreen trees differing from the magnolia in the way its fruits discharge their seeds. There are about 40 species; all are tropical, but they are spread over the Old and New Worlds – they can be seen in tropical and subtropical Asia, southern Mexico, the West Indies, and Brazil. Species of this genus are rarely met in plant collections in the British Isles, but a large vigorous specimen of *Talauma hodgsonii* has been grown under glass at the Royal Botanic Garden, Edinburgh.

Liriodendron

These medium-to-large trees differ from magnolias in their truncate leaves, their differently shaped winter buds, and their closed seed vessels, which contain winged seeds. Two species are widely distributed, one coming from eastern North America and the other from China and Vietnam.

Liriodendron chinense

L. chinense is a medium-to-large tree found across a wide geographical area covering most of the Chinese Provinces of Anhwei, Kiangsi, Fukien, Hupeh, Szechwan, Kweichow, Kwangsi, and Yunnan. It is also found in Thapa, Vietnam.

It was first introduced into the British Isles in 1901 by Ernest Wilson when collecting for Messrs Veitch. Wilson also saw this species on later expeditions of 1907 and 1910, when he was sponsored by the Arnold Arboretum. He found it in Kiangsi and western Hupeh, growing in moist, dense woodlands at altitudes between 3,200ft (975m) and 4,700ft (1,450m).

Trees seen by Ernest Wilson were up to 50ft (15m) in height. Trees in cultivation in southern England can grow taller than 75ft (23m), but they are never as broad-spreading as their American sisters. The green leaves are similar in size to the North American species, having the same truncate apex and the two lateral lobes (but are more deeply lobed than the American species). Like those of its American counterpart, the leaves turn a clear butter yellow in autumn. The flowers, which appear in late June, are smaller and are green outside and yellow inside. The petals, which are about $1\frac{1}{2}$in (3.75cm) long, are probably more widely spread than in the American species.

In the British Isles it grows well in moisture-retentive soils, which can be acid or alkaline. It prefers a sunny site and is rated as US hardiness zones 6 to 7.

Liriodendron tulipifera

This large, broad, spreading tree is native to the deciduous forests of eastern North America, from Massachusetts, Vermont, and southern Ontario southwards to eastern Missouri, Arkansas, Louisiana, and Florida. Generally it grows at low altitudes.

The Tulip Tree or Yellow Poplar was thought to have been introduced into the British Isles by John Tradescant the Younger, who collected extensively in Virginia during 1637, 1642, and 1654 and who brought back the Tulip Tree from one of these expeditions. This makes it one of the earliest introductions to the British Isles; it was being cultivated by Bishop Henry Compton at Fulham Palace in 1688.

The largest plants found in the wild grow in the southern Allegheny Region, where they reach a height of 190ft (58m). Plants in southern England reach a most respectable height, of over 100ft (30.5m), and trees grown in warm, sunny yet sheltered sites elsewhere in the British Isles can also attain good heights. The Tulip Tree has the reputation, especially in its native North America, of being somewhat 'weak wooded' – it casts its limbs during severe weather conditions.

The leaf, which can be up to 8in (20cm) long, has been described as paddle-shaped, because it has two pairs of lateral lobes near the base and two more lobes at the apex, which give it a distinctive truncate appearance. It is bright green above and slightly paler beneath. During the autumn the foliage turns a magnificent butter yellow, probably more of a golden yellow in its native habitats. The flowers are tulip-shaped, about 2in (5cm) tall, pale greenish-yellow on the outside of the petals and pale orange on the inside. They are seen rather sporadically in the British Isles during June and July but more plentifully and earlier, in mid-May and June, in North America. It takes from 10 to 20 years to flower from seed, less time from grafted plants.

A rich, moisture-retentive soil in a sunny yet sheltered site suits the Tulip Tree, which will adjust to either an acid or an alkaline soil. It is perfectly hardy, being quoted as US hardiness zone 5.

The wood is a pale yellow in colour and is used in North America for furniture manufacture. The inner bark of the root is acrid and is used as a stimulant in native medicine. It is also the source of *Tulipiferine*, an alkaloid which acts violently on the heart and nervous system. Tulip Tree honey is reported to be of an excellent quality.

A number of forms of the Tulip Tree are seen in cultivation today:

'Aureomarginatum' is a beautiful variegated-foliage plant which is fairly upright in habit. The yellow margin of the foliage is most distinctive, especially up until midsummer, when it tends to 'green'. A plant in the Hillier Gardens and Arboretum is approaching 50ft (15m) in height after 20 years.

'Fastigiatum' has a good columnar habit and can attain a height of over 60ft (18m), but has a tendency to splay out with age. A similar cultivar to this is 'Arnold' raised at the Arnold Arboretum at Boston. It is an erect columnar form, similar but slower and tighter in growth.

Recommended Species and Varieties

Choosing plants is a personal matter; you can be advised but the choice ultimately rests with you. Listed below are the magnolias that I regard as my favourites. A number of new American hybrids are not mentioned simply because I have not had a chance to grow them, and for no other reason. Many in fact are extremely exciting additions to the magnolia lists and are eagerly awaited in the British Isles. The use of *Magnolia acuminata* has been an interesting choice in a number of hybridizing programmes, with 'Elizabeth' making an impact worldwide. Do not however limit your choice to those mentioned below – you can guarantee that with so many magnolia enthusiasts around, a range of interesting hybrids will be lurking around that corner. On the other side of the coin, do not forget the tried and tested species whose popularity has never been higher.

Medium-sized Shrubs – up to 10ft (3m)
'George Henry Kern', 'Jane', *M. liliiflora* 'Nigra', 'Norman Gould', *M. stellata* 'Centennial', *M. stellata* 'Water Lily', 'Susan'.

Large-sized Shrubs – over 10ft (3m)
M. cylindrica, *M. denudata* 'Purple Eye', 'Elizabeth', 'Freeman', *M.* × *loebneri* 'Leonard Messel', *M. sieboldii*, *M. sinensis*, *M.* × *soulangiana* 'Alba Superba', *M.* × *soulangiana* 'Just Jean', *M.* × *soulangiana* 'Picture', *M.* × *soulangiana* 'San Jose', *M.* × *thompsoniana*, *M.* × *wieseneri*.

Small Crowned Trees – up to 30ft (9m)
'Charles Coates', *M. grandiflora* 'Samuel Sommer', 'Galaxy', 'Heaven Scent', 'Kewensis', *M.* × *loebneri* 'Merrill', 'Peppermint Stick', 'Sayonara', 'Wada's Memory', 'Yellow Lantern'.

Medium Crowned Trees – 35ft (10.5m) to 60ft (18m)
'Albatross', *M. campbellii* var. *mollicomata* 'Lanarth', *M. dawsoniana*, 'Eric Savill', 'Iolanthe', *M. officinalis* var. *biloba*, *M. salicifolia*, *M. sargentiana* var. *robusta*, *M. sprengeri* 'Diva', 'Silver Parasol'.

Large Crowned Trees – over 60ft (19m)
M. acuminata, *M. campbellii*, *M. campbellii* 'Charles Raffill', *M. campbellii* 'Kew's Surprise', *M. hypoleuca*, *M.* × *veitchii* 'Peter Veitch', 'Princess Margaret'.

Magnolias Grown for Flower Scent
'Charles Coates', *M. grandiflora* 'St Mary', *M. hypoleuca*, *M.* × *loebneri* 'Merrill', *M. macrophylla*, *M. officinalis* var. *biloba*, *M. sieboldii*, *M. sinensis*, *M.* × *wieseneri*.

Magnolias Grown for their Foliage Effect
(E = Evergreen, D = Deciduous)
M. delavayi (E), *M. fraseri* (D), *M. grandiflora* 'Samuel Sommer' (E), *M. hypoleuca* (D), *M. macrophylla* (D), *M. nitida* (E), *M. officinalis* var. *biloba* (D), 'Silver Parasol' (D), *M. tripetala* (D).

AWARDS TO MAGNOLIAS

It is easy enough to evaluate the quality of a magnolia's flower (and, often, leaf) by looking at a flower (or foliage) vase on display at one of the British Royal Horticultural Society's Shows. But to judge the plant's other qualities and attributes is more difficult and for these there is no more reliable guide than the awards given by the Royal Horticultural Society. The Awards Committee has before it an accurate assessment of the plant's overall qualities and habit, and so can make a knowledgeable judgement of its merits.

Abbreviations:

AGM	Award of Garden Merit
AM	Award of Merit
CC	Cultural Commendation
FCC	First Class Certificate
PC	Preliminary Commendation

M. 'Ann Rosse'	AM (Nymans 1973)
M. 'Caerhays Surprise'	AM (F. J. Williams 1973)
Magnolia campbellii	FCC (Gumbleton, R. Veitch 1903)
M. campbellii var. *alba*	FCC (C. Williams 1951)
M. c. 'Betty Jessel'	AM (Jessel 1972)
	FCC (Jessel 1975)
M. c. 'Charles Raffill'	PC (Windsor 1959)
	AM (Windsor 1963)
	FCC (Windsor 1966)
M. c. 'Kew's Surprise'	FCC (F. J. Williams 1967)
M. c. 'Queen Caroline'	AM (Kew 1977)
M. c. var. *mollicomata*	FCC (Aberconway 1939)
M. c. var. *mollicomata* 'Mary Williams'	AM (C. Williams 1954)
M. c. var. *mollicomata* 'Lanarth'	FCC (M. P. Williams 1947)
M. 'Charles Coates'	PC (Kew, 1962)
	AM (Windsor 1973)
M. denudata	AGM (1936)
	FCC (1968)
M. denudata 'Purple Eye'	AM (Stevenson Clarke 1926)
M. cylindrica	AM (Windsor 1963)
M. dawsoniana	AM (M. P. Williams 1939)
M. d. 'Chyverton'	AM (N. T. Holman 1974)
M. delavayi	FCC (J. Veitch 1913)
M. 'Eric Savill'	AM (Windsor 1986)
M. fraseri	AM (S. Clarke 1948)
M. globosa	AM (Stair 1931)
M. grandiflora 'Exmouth'	AGM (1969)
M. g. 'Goliath'	AM (Preston 1931)
	FCC (Roberts 1951)
	AGM (1969)
M. hypoleuca	FCC (J. Veitch 1893)
M. h. 'Pink Form' (as *M. officinalis* 'Pink Form')	AM (Windsor 1971)
M. 'Kewensis'	AM (Kew 1952)
M. kobus	AGM (1936)
(as *M. kobus* var. *borealis*)	AM (Price 1948)
	AM (Aberconway 1942)
M. k. 'Nippon'	AM (Collingwood Ingram 1969)
M. liliiflora 'Nigra'	AM (Cuthbert 1907)
	AGM (1969)
	FCC (Simmons 1981)
M. × *loebneri*	AGM (1969)
M. × *loebneri* 'Leonard Messel'	PC (Nymans 1954)
	AM (Nymans 1955)
	FCC (Nymans 1969)
M. × *loebneri* 'Neil McEacharn'	PC (Windsor 1966)
	AM (Windsor 1967)
M. macrophylla	FCC (J. Veitch 1900)
M. 'Michael Rosse'	AM (Nymans 1968)
M. 'Nancy Hardy'	AM (Major A. E. & Mr G. A. Hardy 1984)

M. nitida	AM (F. J. Williams 1966)
M. 'Osaka'	AM (Gauntlett 1902)
M. 'Princess Margaret'	FCC (Windsor 1973)
M. rostrata	AM (Hillier 1974)
M. salicifolia	AM (Rothschild 1927)
	AGM (1941)
	FCC (Windsor 1962)
M. sargentiana	FCC (Messel 1935)
M. s. var. *robusta*	FCC (Aberconway 1947)
M. sieboldii	FCC (J. Veitch 1894)
	AGM (1935)
M. sinensis	AM (Bodnant 1927)
	FCC (R. Veitch 1931)
	AGM (1969)
M. × *soulangiana*	AGM (1932)
M. × *s.* 'Alba Superba'	AGM (1969)
M. × *s.* 'Brozzonii'	FCC (Rothschild 1929)
	AGM (1969)
M. × *s.* 'Lennei'	FCC (Paul 1863)
	AGM (1969)
M. × *s.* 'Norbertii'	AM (Pilkington 1960)
M. × *s.* 'Rustica Rubra'	AM (Pilkington 1960)
	AGM (1969)
M. × *s.* 'San Jose'	AM (Windsor 1986)
M. sprengeri	AM (Aberconway 1942/1947)
M. s. 'Claret Cup'	AM (Aberconway 1963)
M. s. 'Diva'	CC (Upcher 1964)
M. s. var. *elongata*	AM (Aberconway 1955)
M. s. 'Wakehurst'	AM (Price 1948)
M. stellata	FCC (J. Veitch 1878)
	AGM (1923)
M. s. 'Norman Gould'	FCC (Wisley 1967)
M. s. 'Rosea'	AM (J. Veitch 1893)
M. s. 'Rubra'	AM (Notcutt 1948)
M. × *thompsoniana*	AM (Thomas 1958)
M. × *veitchii* 'Peter Veitch'	FCC (R. Veitch 1921)
M. × *wieseneri* (as M. × *watsonii*)	AM (Allgrove 1917)
M. wilsonii	AM (Clarke 1930)
(as *M.* × *highdownensis*)	AM (Loder 1932)
	AM (Stern 1937)
	PC (Windsor 1965)
	FCC (Simmons 1971)
M. 'Wada's Memory'	FCC (Windsor 1986)

Where to See Magnolias

Listed below is a selection of gardens around the world where good collections of magnolias can be found. In order to avoid disappointment, it is always worthwhile contacting garden owners before you visit to ensure that it is convenient to do so.

Belgium

Arboretum Bokrijk, Limburg, B,3600 Gent
Herkenrode, 2990 Wespelaar (Vicomte Philippe de Spoelberch)
Kalmthout Arboretum (R. deBelder)

British Isles

England

Berkshire
The Savill and Valley Gardens, Windsor Great Park (Crown Estate Commissioners)

Cambridgeshire
University Botanic Garden, Cambridge

Cheshire
Ness Gardens, Neston, South Wirral (University of Liverpool)

Cornwall
Anthony House, Torpoint (National Trust)
Caerhays Castle, Gorran, St Austell (Mr F. J. Williams)
Chyverton, Zelah, Truro (Mr and Mrs M. V. Holman)
Glendurgan, Mawnan Smith, Falmouth (National Trust)
Lanhydrock, Bodmin (National Trust)
Penwarne, Mawnan Smith, Falmouth (Mr and Mrs H. Beister)
Tregothnam, Truro (The Viscount Falmouth)
Trellissick, Truro (National Trust)
Trengwainton, Penzance (National Trust)
Trewidden, Penzance (Executors of the late Mrs Charles Williams)
Trewithen, Grampound Road, Truro (Mrs G. H. Johnston)
Werrington Park, Launceston (Mr. A. M. Williams)

Devon
Dartington Hall Gardens, Totnes (Dartington Hall Trust)
The Garden House, Buckland Monachorum, Yelverton (The Fortescue Garden Trust)
Killerton Gardens, Exeter (National Trust)
Sharpitor Gardens, Salcombe (National Trust)

Dorset
Abbotsbury Gardens, Weymouth (Strangeways Estate)

Gloucestershire
The Batsford Arboretum, Moreton in Marsh (The Lord Dulverton)

Hampshire
Exbury Gardens, Beaulieu (Edmond de Rothschild)
The Hillier Gardens and Arboretum, Romsey (Hampshire County Council)

Kent
Sandling Park, Hythe (Mr and Mrs G. Hardy)

Norfolk
Talbot Manor, Fincham (Mr Maurice Mason)

Surrey
The Royal Botanic Gardens, Kew, Richmond
Tilgates, Bletchingley (Mr David Clulow)
Wisley Gardens, Ripley (Royal Horticultural Society)

Sussex
Nymans Gardens, Handcross (National Trust)
Wakehurst Place, Ardingly (Royal Botanic Gardens, Kew)

Yorkshire
Castle Howard, York (The Hon Simon Howard)

Scotland

Argyll
Arduaine Gardens, Loch Melfort (Mr H. Wright)
Brodick Castle Gardens, The Isle of Arran (National Trust for Scotland)
Kiloran, The Island of Colonsay (The Lord Strathcona and the Mount Royal)

Edinburgh
The Royal Botanic Garden, Edinburgh

Wigtonshire
Logan Botanic Gardens, Stranraer (Royal Botanic Garden, Edinburgh)

Wales

Gwynedd
Plas Newydd, Isle of Anglesey (National Trust)
Bodnant Gardens, Tal-y-Cafn (National Trust)

Ireland

County Cork
Fota Island, Carrigtwohill (Richard Wood/University College, Cork)

County Down
Rowallane Gardens, Saintfield (National Trust)

County Dublin
Mount Usher

County Offaly
Birr Castle (Lord Rosse)

County Waterford
Mount Congreve, Waterford (Ambrose Congreve)

County Wexford
Dunloe Castle Hotel (Killarney Hotels Ltd)

Canada

British Columbia
University of British Columbia Botanical Garden, Vancouver V6T 1W5

China
Hangzhou Botanical Garden (Municipal)
Kunming Botanical Garden (Academia Sinica)
Guilin Botanical Garden (Guangxi Academy of Sciences)
Nanyue Arboretum (The Forestry Bureau of Hunnan)

Denmark
Universitets Botaniske Have, Farmimagsgade, Copenhagen

Federal German Republic
Frankfurter Palmenggarten, Frankfurt

France
Fondations de Parks de France, 45450 Fay-aux-Loges (Count Bernard de Rochefoucauld)
Jardin Botanique de la Ville, Nantes (Municipal)
Pépinières de kerisnel, St. Pol-de-Leon (Société d'Initiatives et de Cooperation Agricoles Sica)
Le Vasterival, F76119 Varengeville-sur-mer (Princess G. Sturdza)

Italy
Issola Bella, Lago di Maggiore
Ville Taranto, Pallanze, Lago di Maggiore (Municipal)

Japan
Koshigaya, Aritaki Arboretum (T. Aritaki)

Korea
Chollipo Arboretum, Chungchong Nando (Ferris Miller)

Netherlands
Doorn, Arboretum Gimborn (University of Utrecht)

Poland
Kornick, Polish Academy of Sciences (Governmental)

Sweden
Botaniska Tradgarden, S41319 Goteborg
Karlstad (A. Blomqvist)
Norrauramov, S26700 Bjuu (K. E. Flinck)
Vasteras (T. Widenfalk)

Switzerland
Veytaux 1820 (K. E. Flinck)
Vico Morcote, Lugano (Sir Peter Smithers)
Vira Gambarogno (Dr P. van Veen)

U.S.S.R.
Batumi Botanical Garden (Georgian Academy of Sciences)

United States of America

Alabama
3961 Cottage Hill Road, Mobile 36609 (Dr J. A. Smith)

California
Los Angeles State and County Arboretum, Arcadia CA 91006
Strybing Arboretum, San Francisco, CA 94122
H. E. Huntington Library, San Marina CA 91108
Saratoga Horticultural Foundation, CA 95070

Delaware
Henry F. DuPont Garden, Winterthur

Georgia
Callaway Gardens, Pine Mountains 31822

Illinois
Chicago Horticultural Society Botanic Garden, Glencoe 60022
University of Illinois, Urbana 61801

Massachusetts
Arnold Arboretum of Harvard University, Boston 02130

Michigan
2150 Woodward Avenue, Bloomfield Hills, 48013

Mississippi
Gloster Arboretum, Gloster 39638

Missouri
Missouri Botanical Garden, St Louis 36110

New Jersey
The Arboretum of Rutgers University, Gladstone 07935

New York
Brooklyn Botanic Garden, Brooklyn 11225
The Cary Arboretum, Millbrook 12545

Pennsylvania
Gardens of the Henry Foundation, Gladwyne 19035
Morris Arboretum, Philadelphia 19118

Tennessee
Great Smoky Mountains National Park, Gatlinburg 37738

Washington, D.C
U.S. National Arboretum, Washington, D.C. 20002

SUPPLIERS

Australia

W. J. Simpson, Wayside, 602 Nepean Highway, Franston, Victoria 3199

British Isles

Bodnant Garden Nursery, Tal-y-cafn, Clywd LL28 5RE

Bridgemere Garden World, Nantwich, Cheshire

Burncoose and Southdown Nurseries, Redruth, Cornwall TR16 6BJ

Crown Estate Commissioners, Savill Gardens, Windsor, Berks SL4 2HT

Fortescue Garden Trust, Buckland Monachorum, Devon PL20 7LQ

Hillier Nurseries (Winchester) Ltd, Romsey, Hampshire SO51 9PA

Knightshayes Garden Trust, Tiverton, Devon EX16 7RG

The Lanhydrock Gardens, Bodmin, Cornwall PL30 5AD

Mallet Court Nursery, Taunton, Somerset TA3 6SY

Notcutts Nurseries Ltd, Woodbridge, Suffolk IP12 4AF

Pickard's Magnolia Gardens, Canterbury, Kent CT3 4AG

Rosemoor Gardens, Torrington, Devon EX2 7JY

Spinners, Lymington, Hampshire SO41 5QE

Trehane Camellia Nursery, Wimborne, Dorset BH21 7NE

Trewithen Nurseries, Truro, Cornwall TR2 4DD

Canada

Ocean Park Nurseries, 2124 Stevenson Road, White Rock, British Columbia.

Netherlands

Firma C. Esveld, Rijneveld 72, 2771 X. S. Boskoop

New Zealand

Duncan and Davis Ltd., P. O. Box 340, New Plymouth Taranaki

Oswald Blumhardt, No. 9 Road, Whangarei

United States of America

Gossler Farms Nursery, 1200 Weaver Road, Springfield, Oregon 97477

Greer Gardens, 1280 Good Pasture, Island Road, Eugene, Oregon 97401–1794

Kluis Nursery, Ryan Road, Malboro, New Jersey 67746

Lousiana Nursery, Route 7, Box 43, Opelousas, Louisiana 70570

Magnolia Nursery and Display Gardens, Route 1, Box 87, Chunchulia, Alabama 36521

Tom Dodd Nurseries, U.S. Highway 98, Semmes, Alabama 36575

Societies

The International Registrar of Magnolia Cultivars,
Arnold Arboretum,
Jamaica Plain,
Boston, Massachusetts 02130,
U.S.A. (Peter Del Tredici)

The Magnolia Society,
907 S. Chestnut Street,
Hammond, Louisiana 70403–5102,
U.S.A. (Phelan A. Bright)

The Rhododendron and Camellia Group (with Magnolias),
The Royal Horticultural Society,
Vincent Square,
London SW1P 2PE,
England

Bibliography

Of the many books on the magnolia and its allies that have been published in Britain and the United States, the following are indispensable for the enthusiast's bookshelf. Neil Treseder's book, in particular, is highly recommended – it is packed with detailed information.

Johnstone, G. H., *Asiatic Magnolias in Cultivation*, 1955
Millais, J. G., *Magnolias*, 1927
Royal Horticultural Society, *Camellias and Magnolias*, Conference Report, 1950
Treseder, N. D., *Magnolias*, 1978

ACKNOWLEDGEMENTS

I would like to thank a number of people without whose help, support, and guidance this book would not have been written. Roy Lancaster gave me, initially, the chance to say no to writing this book and, subsequently, horticultural advice, guidance, and photographs. Vincent Page made the necessary arrangements and offered sound advice on the content. Philip J. Savage wrote the Foreword to this edition. John Gallagher (whose photographs speak for themselves) offered expert advice on plants, gave guidance on the book's contents, read through the manuscript, and made valuable comments. Wendy Butler and Dr Ken Robertson have both made significant contributions. Allen Coombes, Bill George, Lenarth Jonsson, Karl Flinck, John Hillier, Lord Howick, and Tony Schilling all provided horticultural information and Chris Watts contributed meteorological data.

My especial thanks to Graham Adcock and Peter Dummer of Hillier Nurseries for advice on propagation and to Rita Farrell, Chris Lane, and Phillip McMillan Browse for information on specific techniques. My thanks, too, to Hampshire County Council, for maintaining at the Hillier Gardens and Arboretum a substantial collection of magnolias to which I have frequently referred.

Most important of all, an especial thank you to my wife Allison, who led a lonely life while I was burning the midnight oil, and to Jillian and Andrew who, at five and three years respectively, must be the country's youngest magnolia experts.

PICTURE CREDITS

Vincent Page pp. 33, 34, 47, 49(top), 52, 55(bottom left), 58, 64(top), 65(bottom), 66–7, 68, 69, 71, 72(bottom), 73(bottom), 74–5, 76(top), 76(bottom), 78–9, 80(top), 80(bottom), 82, 84–5, 90–91; Jim Gardiner pp. 35(top), 49(bottom), 55(bottom left), 60(top), 72(top), 73(top), 76, 81, 82–3, 86(top), 86(bottom), 87; Hampshire County Council pp. 35(bottom), 69(top), 56(bottom), 59, 62–3; John Gallagher pp. 36–7, 38(bottom), 40–41, 43(bottom), 44–5, 46, 48, 50, 50–51, 52(top), 52(bottom), 54, 55(top), 57(bottom), 64(bottom), 70–71, 92(top), 92 (bottom left), 92(bottom right), 93, 94(top left), 94(top right), 94(centre), 94(bottom right), 95; John Hillier pp. 39(top), 65(top); Roy Lancaster pp. 39(bottom), 61, 88, 89, 91, 96; Tony Schilling pp. 42, 43(top); Dr Ken Robertson pp. 56(top), 57(top), 60(bottom).

INDEX

Numbers in *italics* refer to the captions to the colour plates. **Bold** numbers refer to the main entry in which the species or hybrid is comprehensively described.

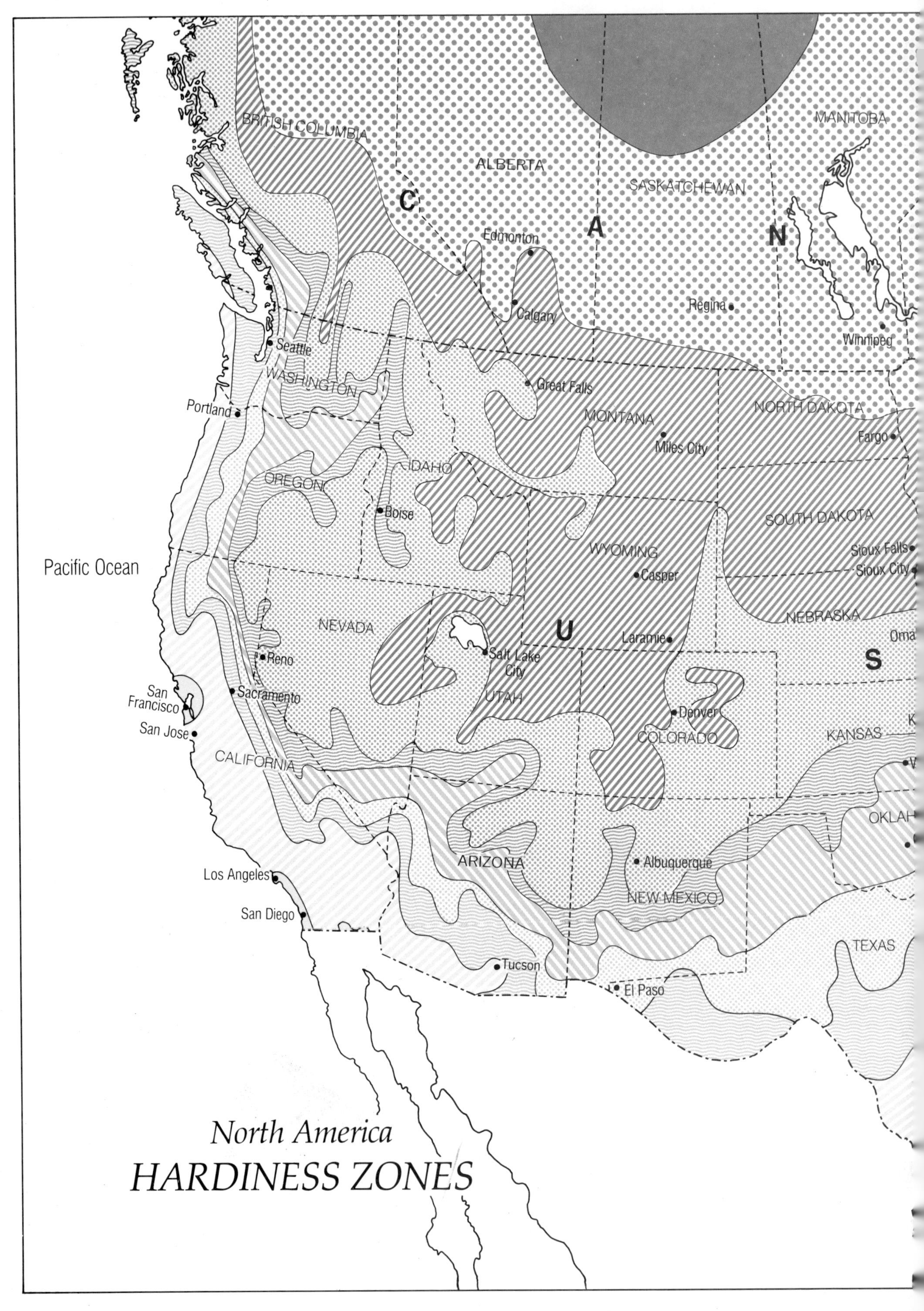

BRITISH COLUMBIA
ALBERTA
SASKATCHEWAN
MANITOBA
C
A
N
Edmonton
Calgary
Regina
Winnipeg
Seattle
WASHINGTON
Portland
Great Falls
MONTANA
NORTH DAKOTA
Miles City
Fargo
IDAHO
OREGON
Boise
SOUTH DAKOTA
WYOMING
Sioux Falls
Sioux City
Casper
Pacific Ocean
NEVADA
NEBRASKA
U
Laramie
Reno
Salt Lake City
S
UTAH
San Francisco
Sacramento
Denver
San Jose
COLORADO
KANSAS
CALIFORNIA
ARIZONA
Albuquerque
Los Angeles
NEW MEXICO
San Diego
TEXAS
Tucson
El Paso
North America
HARDINESS ZONES